Skid

Row

Blues

Why America's Ghettos

Should Be Destroyed

by

NNMS

Skid Row Blues

ISBN-13 978-1718949553
ISBN-10 1718949553

1. Sociology 2. True Crime 3. NNMS

Printed and/or electronically distributed in the United States of America

First Edition September, 2018

In memory of my

father James L. 1942-2018

CHAPTER ONE

The floor in my cell is freezing cold. Thick concrete walls keep the heat of the Los Angeles sun out, and the smell is like that of a gas station bathroom. The guards yelled at me to put my arms back through my sleeves, so even though I try to warm myself I can't. The shoes they gave me are two sizes too small and come off every time I walk the four flights of stairs to the cafeteria. L.A. county jail is probably the worst in the country.

Despite the horrible food, sadistic guards, endless noise, and a wide outbreak of the flesh-eating bacteria STAPH on every bedroll, there is a more pressing reason to be afraid. The black and Mexican gangs are at war, and attacks go on daily. The dorm I'm in holds about three hundred people, enough for a pretty big disturbance. I had been living near downtown Los Angeles for almost two years, so while going through processing I saw at least a dozen people I knew and fifty other faces I recognized.

They were all gangsters, dealers, dopers, hustlers, and boosters. If you knew someone's face and you weren't enemies on the street, it was a good idea to say hello and do that to as many people as possible while going through processing. You'll see a thousand people over the three days it takes to be processed as you go through the horrific maze of lowly paid jailhouse workers taking fingerprints, filling out paperwork, issuing ID bracelets, and taking blood. There's safety in numbers, and everybody knew it.

Processing takes days, and everyone deals with the shock in their own way. You are either in a cell waiting to move to another location or waiting to see someone that has something to do with the intake process. I had just shot up four bags before getting arrested, so I decided not to stress about my ordeal and enjoy my high. I sat at the rampart division chained to a wall, nodding off and singing to myself. I knew I was fucked, and there was no way out. You're there for the next few days, so you might as well chill.

The next morning all of the dope addicts start to kick. The junkies I knew and I huddled in a small circle, freezing our asses of f and wondering which of us had to swallow their balloons. If you swallowed any balloons while getting arrested, you're going to experience the joy of holding a napkin or hand if nothing else is available under your butt to collect the shit that you must dig through to find the balloons. Usually by that time you've got diarrhea and you had better hope you have a plastic baggie big enough to collect your waste, because the watery discharge coming out means you had to pray that the balloons don't somehow get past your hand and wind up in the bowl where every homeless person in Los Angeles has expelled their waste.

If that happens, you're going to have to stick your hand in that hepatitis infested water and dig around for it and there are no plastic gloves. You might get lucky and be in a cell with a toilet that flushes, but probably not. This means the waste of the rest of the people who have been brought in today will be in the bowl. I have truly been fortunate to not have to dig through that pile, but I have seen people do it.

That's how strong the addiction is. It feels like you can't breathe and you WILL stick your hand in that bowl and dig around for as long as it takes. You have no choice. For me there is no hope. It's Saturday morning, and the EARLIEST possible time you can see the judge is Monday morning, so we knew we were in for a ride. Kicking dope anywhere else in the world is a little more selfish. You can thrash around, scream, plot and plan an escape to get dope, or at least fantasize about it. Kicking dope in jail is different. There is no leeway and no one feels sorry for you.

There were guys who had been bitching all night and all morning and tempers were short. It didn't take long for them to get a beat down. We all suffer the same indignities. It's okay to tell people you're kicking heroin but externalizing the pain verbally is not appreciated by anyone. I rolled up in a ball, bit my lips, and suffered in silence.

If you're lucky, you can find enough space on the floor to lie down, otherwise you're stuck sitting on a hard metal bench. Worse yet, it could be standing room only or you could break your back leaning against the metal bars. They're always overcrowded, and people never shut up. Anyone who smuggled drugs in will be doing them, and there is no way in hell they will share unless you have something of value to trade, and since we were in processing, all of our possessions were taken.

Eventually the guards came in to feed us. We were given a microwaveable burrito, still in the plastic wrap and heated to three hundred degrees. I couldn't eat mine, but I stuffed it in my pants and felt the warmth of it stave off the chills for half an hour. I know I should eat something but I just can't. We spend a few hours going through fingerprinting and mug shots and I got to see mine. My skin was a yellowish green and my eyes looked like two billiard table pockets. I remember being repulsed at the sight of my own photograph, incarcerated, dope sick, unshowered and unshaven, and thinking about how terrible I looked.

Sooner or later they transport you from the police station to the county jail. The cop reads a list of all of the people who are to be taken to county, and when he starts talking everyone yells, "RADIO! RADIO THAT SHIT!! instead of "SHUT THE FUCK UP!!" Yelling "SHUT UP!" at people started too many fights, so someone came up with yelling 'radio' instead. It worked. They separate everyone by race, blacks are chained to blacks, and Whites and Latinos go together, another way to stop fights. Once you are shackled hand and foot, they

herd you on to the bus to deliver you to Dante's second level
of hell.

CHAPTER TWO

You don't feel so ashamed in jail. Everyone else there is busted and the guards are akin to Nazi Stormtroopers so you wouldn't even be able to identify with them on the outside. None of your friends or family can see you, so you loosen up a bit after the initial shock. They even turned the radio on the bus up, and here we were, sixty of L.A.'s worst, singing along at full volume, "I got sunshiiiine, on a cloudy daaaaaay, When it's coooold outsiiiide, I got the month of Maaaaay." We bobbed our heads along with the music, some guys did the harmonies, and we all laughed for a bit.

When we got to county it was a different story. You're herded into a holding cell with no chairs, no bathroom, and huge plexiglass windows all around. You're in there for at least six hours and there were speed freaks all around me screaming incomprehensibly. At one point they brought the female prisoners past our cell, backed them up against the wall, and proceeded to strip search them for forty minutes. It was done to totally demoralize them because our faces were pressed against the glass arguing about which one was the hottest; there were the typical homeless women, then middle aged women who dressed a bit nicer to shoplift, but some of the girls they brought in were downright beauties.

Eventually we got moved along into another holding cell where we were searched. We stood against a big wall in a corridor, took off each item of clothing and shook it out. The guards snapped on rubber gloves; this was where some of the inmates started to get nervous. Nobody likes being touched. Most of the beatings I've seen in there were dished out by guards. All were brutal, and maybe one out of ten was severe. Soon they had everyone touching their toes and one guard went up and down the line with a flashlight looking into everyone's anal region and telling people to cough. I did not envy his position one bit.

This is a system set up to ensure the total subversion of human beings and it has been studied over the years in war and in peace. Isolating men from their friends and families, crowding them into pens and making them suffer indignities makes them more compliant, easier to bend, and definitely messes with their heads. The inner conflict is that they fuck with you. If you fight back, which is a natural instinct when someone fucks with you, your time is extended for small infractions. In order to be able to be released as quickly as possible you must take whatever shit they dish out. They make sure you know that they are in charge and this is their house.

The problem to this approach is twofold. One of the detrimental effects is on the men, but the other is the effect it has is on society. In the 60's an experiment was set up in the basement of the Stanford University psychology department. After it was over and the results were published it became one of the most infamous and telling psychological experiments in history.

Two teams of young men were chosen and asked to stay for the weekend. The experiment was held in the lower underground floors of a typical college building. Several large rooms were on both sides of a corridor, ample space for the twenty or so students involved in the project. The teams were chosen at random, half of the students were guards and half were prisoners.

The prisoners were given drab clothing that resembled jailhouse uniforms. The guards were given proper uniforms that were clean and pressed. All of the guards had police style hats, badges on their uniforms, and polished black hard soled shoes that gave a clunk clunk along the floors as they walked, making their steps seem more important than the prisoners, who wore rubber toed soles to keep their footsteps quiet. The approach of boots is an alarming sound that has been written about in history after history of the world. It has a deep damaging psychological effect on anyone in the way.

During the first day, the prisoners were herded into different cells, the police were told to be stern, but not harmful to the prisoners in any way. After the first night, both the guards and the prisoners were allowed to start embellishing the stories that were going on and create their own rules.

That's when the administrator noticed some very strange behavior in both parties. Despite being in a cardboard jail, the prisoners made no attempt to leave, as if the bars were permanent and made of iron instead of drawn on the window with a sharpie. One student was so badly traumatized that he had to return home after being excused from the experiment. He had a total breakdown while in the classroom from the taunting of the guards, and instead of quitting or walking out, he sat down in the room and had an anxiety attack.

Only one prisoner the entire weekend demanded to be released, the rest took abuse after abuse and the guards got more and more severe in their behavior. There was also a noticeable change in the ruthlessness of the guards once they issued themselves mirrored sunglasses, which they wore in the cells as well as the halls. By the end, the guards were making the prisoners eat food of fof the floor. The administrator was so upset that he ended the experiment and sent everyone home.

CHAPTER THREE

The resemblance between Skid Row and a prison is no accident. Keeping people fighting with each other because they are crammed into the tiniest of spaces keeps them from turning on their captors. This is how jails and prisons are designed and how they are able to keep the most amount of people under control with the least amount of guards.

They remove all color and mental stimulation from the prison, all books, paper, music, creative or decorative tools, and paint the walls a stark and forlorn color. They remind you constantly that THEY are in control, and herd inmates into line after line, always making sure to open and close every door with a loud BANG. People are crowded into smaller and smaller pens, making them more and more stressed each time they are given an even more crowded room to try and sleep or be comfortable in. On Skid Row, people are in rooms so close to each other that you can't help feeling that if you can hear the people next door, they can hear (and are listening to!) YOU.

The doorways that line the streets of Skid Row have little to no detail or color on them. If there is anything on it to read, it is in a sterile metal font embedded in the doorway. The buildings are drab and square and there is garbage everywhere. Though it is an open area, people who stay here for more than three years are considered chronically homeless and given extra privileges. They can apply for section 8 housing, medical and dental insurance, insurance for eyewear and eye health appointments, and the benefits are not small.

In other words, upon landing in Skid Row and meeting with a social worker, you quickly find out that by not having a job and having a little bit of paperwork savvy, in three short years you will qualify for a FREE apartment! Section 8 housing isn't exactly shabby either. By California state law, each town must have a certain percentage of section 8 housing available to those who are in need.

This makes it easy for the towns to get certain tax breaks and incentives, but the only problem is NO ONE wants the homeless to be in their neighborhood. Now, there certainly are people who are in desperate need of this housing, and I am not an expert on what or how people are qualified for these apartments but I DO see who gets them, what their lives are like before they qualify and I have NO faith in this system for either being fair or a benefit to the state in any way.

This method of choosing and giving out apartments to people in need is certainly better than not doing anything at all, but it gives a 'jackpot' style of benefit awarding that reminds me of a lottery. If your name is on a list, you might never be called or you might get an apartment right away, there is no way to tell where you are on the list and who or why a person gets chosen. It is supposed to be based on the most dire need, but the residents of the towns that these people soon come to reside in create a panic amongst homeowners in other towns, who then do everything they can to stop the 'most qualified people' from getting into their beloved and beautiful coastal community.

In my case I had applied for an apartment in the beautiful coastal city of Redondo Beach. I was sure I was one of the first to sign up as soon as this building announced it was going to have some vacancies. After a few weeks I did some followups to see if I was going to be considered for one of these apartments, and sure enough, they were all taken. I did some searching, and it turns out that the apartments all went to friends and relatives of Redondo Beach residents. They had formerly lived in retirement communities, with their families, in hospitals, and now they all had their own apartments paid for by the State of California.

It is certainly a sign of good health for a community to be able to provide for their ill, their wounded, their homeless and their unloved and unwanted, but it also is detrimental to the people who have put a HUGE amount of work into making their town as peaceful and clean as it is before the homeless came along.

I won't mention any towns in particular, but I will relate a story of what happened in a town not far from mine in

Orange County. This is a worst case scenario, and having the homeless move into housing is certainly one of the benefits of civilization. It also shows a sense of common its pride as well as a sense of security for those who visit. The homeless aren't on the street corners begging for change and pissing in the gutters, they are in an apartment complex that provides shelter, food in many cases, and a minimal amount of assistance should they need it.

This is all very well and good, and certainly decided on in council meeting after council meeting with the best of intentions, however it doesn't always go as planned. The homeless who move into these section 8 houses and apartments are usually people with mental illnesses (though like myself, being in recovery applies as a 'mental disability' and the people are often demonized for something that isn't really going to bother anyone).

There are however, too many people with mental illnesses that WILL result in them bothering people in the towns, and one person living in section 8 housing with a bad attitude can really ruin the best intentions for thousands of people.

An older woman whom I helped move into her Section 8 apartment immediately started accosting people in the street who lived in the apartment building nearby, telling stories about shootings, assaults from people climbing in her window, and other fun things that made everyone want to get as far away from her as possible. Another person upon moving into his new section 8 home started acting out as if he were still in prison, accosting anyone within striking distance and accusing them of stealing from him, being extremely aggressive and belligerent, and making everyone nervous and fearful that he might physically attack them.

Taking a person out of prison, out of a mental hospital, or of fof the streets of Skid Row, all places where they must defend themselves constantly, and placing them into a quiet, charming, beautiful coastal village is often causing more harm than it does good. It has all the best intentions of the people in the city, but over time, it creates a backlash against the people who desperately need this kind of help. After a few well publicized stories like the ones I just mentioned, add in one murder or child abduction that could happen anywhere in the country (and has nothing to do with the people who are trying to get off of the streets, but still attaches itself to their story), and you have the perfect storm of intolerance that has plagued the homeless from the beginning.

The real scary thing is that the people who commit most of these crimes are actually the ones who are able to hide the best and can shake off any suspicion with well rehearsed tales of how noble and valiant they are, therefore nullifying any real evidence that may have been built up against them. It never allows the stigma of homelessness to be wiped away from the people who have experienced it, unless they are able to completely change their image and create a persona that no one can image as homeless.

The elderly, people who have severe injuries or diseases, many people who have physical and mental disabilities, ex convicts with 'prison mentality' and the impoverished are not as able to shake of ftheir homeless characteristics quite so easily and therefore they are often stuck with the prejudice and hatred that accompany attitudes towards the homeless. The real sadness here is that the people who are able to work but have given up or been too beaten down to keep trying are the ones who cause the most damage.

I have known people who have distinct medical disabilities, badly need assisted living care, and might have a family that relies on them to at least not be a burden on their stretched resources. Those are the people these apartments SHOULD go to, and how they differentiate one from the other completely escapes me, It seems MOST of the people who are granted these luxury apartments are people who fool the person who decides if they are qualified. These myths and methods are passed around Skid Row until they are no longer useful or have been heard too many times.

This means that people can be REWARDED for not trying to climb out of homelessness, rewarded for being a criminal, rewarded for wasting their life in a way that makes them easy to control. For three years while waiting to see if they get chosen for a nice section 8 apartment, they will be on the streets, in and out of jail, using and creating a demand for drugs and giving back every dime that they make.

There are many cases of people who are simply unable to work for whatever reason and legitimately need help, but my estimate is that maybe fifteen percent of all who apply are actually qualified and in need. The other eighty five percent are people who have either simply given up (and given up WAY too easily!), don't WANT to work or become a contributing member of society, have an alternate source of income that is illegal and therefore not on any record in the state and therefore the state shows them as homeless, or are simply clever enough to work the system and patient enough to make it worthwhile to wait for this perceived gold mine to come through for them.

The other thing to remember is that these apartments are not guaranteed; they are handed out by the city that the apartment building is located in and the residents get little to no choice as to where they might wind up. Simply having your name on a list is never enough. I applied for one as a student, but also being in recovery qualified me for a disability.

The building I wanted was located by the ocean, or at least in a town close enough that getting to the shore was within walking or bike riding distance. Where I currently live in downtown Los Angeles made it difficult and time consuming to get to the ocean. Last year they opened up a much anticipated Metro train stop in Santa Monica, right on the boardwalk. This meant that anyone in the downtown area could hop on one train and be at the ocean in forty minutes. This was a boon for tourism as well as residents who could now live in many more places and still have easy access to the ocean.

Before this new seaside station was completed it took one train and two buses to get to the ocean, which included Venice beach, Marina Del Rey, and Santa Monica, not to mention buses that ran up and down Pacific Coast Highway, giving you easy access to places like Malibu, Redondo Beach, and other coastal towns. This made it VERY difficult for people visiting from out of town to get to the ocean. Today, one train goes right from downtown to the Santa Monica shore, and it's perfect. I love it.

It's simple enough to qualify and get on a list, all you have to do is sign up at one of the homeless shelters in Los Angeles and give them your legal information. With the ID card that they give you, make sure to check in once in a while so that you can prove that you have been staying at the shelter. If you fuck up and get a job, you have to wait for another three years, because you are automatically sent to the end of the line. That's a gross oversimplification of how the process works, but again, the people who know it best are the ones who are homeless yet sitting in a paid for luxury apartment right now.

Those buildings get turned into a den of snakes; drug dealers often take over a resident's apartment and threaten them into having to let their place be used as a central location for crack smoking and dealing, prostitution, or worse. THIS is why most people try and keep them out of their towns, not because of the homeless or invalid; not because of the people with mental or emotional disabilities, and not because of the poverty that others fear is contagious.

It's the predators that prey on them. It's the people who look for easy targets and follow the homeless wherever they go, knowing that they are the most easily talked into buying their drugs, or selling their bodies to buy drugs. They know the people who get these apartments are easily threatened and intimidated, and will give up their own security at the slightest sign of danger. It's also convenient for the impoverished to be cramped into concentration camp like ghettos so that dealers and predators have more people in their territory.

All too often the predators are not gang members, they are not pimps and pushers, or ex-convicts that try to steal and coerce those with weaknesses they know about. All too often the predators are judges, lawyers, teachers, civil service workers, and worst of all, police.

This is another part of the mentality that they enforce upon the poor in the United States. When I lived in Chicago, the highest crime neighborhood in the city, Cabrini

Greene, was built right in the middle of the expensive North Shore. Anyone living in the Cabrini projects had to drive through neighborhoods filled with expensive cafes, posh boutiques, and high rent brownstone apartments to get home.

Naturally, impoverished criminals went to where the money was. It was common for muggers to drive up into the neighborhoods adjacent to the projects, jump out and steal someone's belongings while they walk in one of the nearby neighborhoods then dash back into the safety of the projects before the police even arrived. The effect this had was to create tension between the people who lived in the Cabrini Greene projects and the people who lived in the affluent North Shore.

Obversely, wealthy criminals went into the Cabrini Greene projects, neglected security, build substandard housing, cut corners on sanitation, building materials, and workmanship, and again, this created tension. Today Skid Row is within arm's length of the financial district, giant banks with bold, glowing lights, and well dressed men and women, smiling and talking endlessly on their phones and eating at fancy restaurants, all while the homeless look in from the outside and dream of better days.

CHAPTER FOUR

They shined flashlights in our faces, in our mouths, under our balls, and between the cheeks as we coughed. If you were suspect, one of those rubber gloves went up your ass. Even though they did find a few bags of dope in some of the guys, we felt bad for them. Who expects you to voluntarily turn over dope you've got in your butt? Combine that with the indignity of being singled out in front of your comrades, and your pride went right out the window. Combine THAT with the knowledge you're about to get some serious time added to your sentence (possession inside of the jail could mean three years) and you've got a very bad situation for the poor guy.

Next, they march you to get your prison clothes, baggy blue shirts and pants with used boxer shorts and shoes that look like they were a third grader's school project. You can't put it on yet because you've got to take a shower, which I wasn't looking forward to because I was already freezing from heroin withdrawal. I was anxious to get in, mostly because I smelled like shit but I also wanted to get into some fresh clothes. The way they screamed at us and marched us from room to room made me think of books I've read on concentration camps.

They led us into a room that had four huge holding cells and six long metal benches that held about fifty guys each, sitting front to back. The room was already full, and God knows what was at the end of it. All I knew was that it was going to take all night to get through.

They actually came through with something I could eat this time, peanut butter and jelly sandwiches. They gave you two pieces of wheat bread and a package with a good amount of jelly and one with enough peanut butter to make it into a football. The worst part was the lowest bidder government contracted fruit juice supplier, which was supposed to be some kind of orange drink but tasted like sugary piss. I gladly wolfed down the sandwich and saw a few more people I knew in line. We were allowed to talk whenever we weren't being transferred.

After a few hours I got to the front of the line. I was ordered to go to a window where a funky looking civilian black lady with bright red Jamaican braids, ornately custom painted Lee press on tiger claws, and a cotton oxford shirt sat. She looked bored beyond comprehension to be there.

"Are you taking any medication?"

"No, but I'm going through Heroin withdrawal so any medication you could give me would help?".

"So, you want to see the doctor?"

"Yes, please."

"Okay sir, we'll let you see him."

I thought I had it made. I thought the door would be opened and some first-year intern would listen to my sad, whiny, bitchy little story and give me enough sleeping pills and anti-diarrhea medicine to knock me out for the rest of the week. I knew they wouldn't give me methadone. In jail you lay in your bed all day long and I'd rather sleep through my withdrawal than suffer through it. I couldn't have been more wrong. I was told to go back out, and I saw a friend of mine in the holding cell.

"What happened?"

"They're going to let me see the doctor, I told them I was kicking."

"WHAT?!?!! They're going to send you to the psych ward now!! You won't get to see the doctor for three days! That's just three more days you gotta be here!! Besides, he won't give you shit!! It's state law for all incoming prisoners to see a doctor if they request it!"

FUCK! I ran back into the room and told the lady, "I'm okay, I don't need to see the doctor, really so can you take my name off of the list?"

"Sir, I'm sorry, but once you ask to see him, we're legally liable for you. Only the doctor at this point can decide if you can be released or not."

"But I was just in here! Forget everything I said!"

She wasn't buying it. I had been counting on seeing the judge on Monday morning. Anything could happen in court no matter what your crime was and I was a sweet-talking defendant. There may be just too many people in the county jail and they HAVE to release some. You could get time served and released that day. Either way, I had officially fucked myself. I wasn't going to see the judge until at LEAST Thursday morning. That was three more days I had to go through withdrawal.

CHAPTER FIVE

We moved into another holding cell, and I spent another torturous night with a burrito in my pants. At least this cell had a toilet, and all of the dope addicts were getting diarrhea from withdrawal. It was pretty gross, but at least we had a place to go. They feed you breakfast at about two-thirty in the morning. All night long cell doors are slammed shut as hard as possible, lights are left on full blast and there's no way you can get comfortable. It makes everyone sleepy all day long, and when you're sleepy, you're less likely to start shit with an inmate or guard. It's all part of the process to keep you docile through sleep deprivation.

At the beginning of our third day we all had bags under our eyes, weren't talking anywhere near as much and shuffled along at half speed. We still had one more day of processing and then we could get assigned a bunk- then we could sleep. The process took three torturous days and nights and I later found out they used the same techniques on prisoners of war in the middle east.

A few years after I was incarcerated and went through this process, the ACLU came to the county jail and filed a lawsuit against them saying that moving inmates from cell to cell for days at a time is a human rights violation and all inmates must be assigned a bunk for the duration of their stay as soon as they enter the building.

Today processing takes between four to eight hours.

Sometime in the early morning we walked up four flights of stairs, down four flights of stairs and through a maze of hallways. I started to notice all of the propaganda painted on the concrete walls. The jails were run by the sheriff's department, so there were paintings of sheriffs in their pressed green uniforms and their almost cowboy hats on every wall. The next wall would have a painting of an L.A. county sherif fholding on to a little girl's hand walking her safely across the road. They even had one of a sheriff carrying a little old lady's bag of groceries. The best one was a huge mural of John Wayne in a sheriff's uniform with his ten-gallon cowboy hat on.

A cop bashed my leg with his flashlight as I had started to doze off. My ass hurt from sitting on those steel benches so long. I was miserable but getting thrashed with a Maglite was worse. I was hallucinating at that point, and spots and flying saucers clouded my vision.

The nurse took one look at my arms and said, "Ummm, your veins are collapsed. Are you sure you don't have any abscesses?"

I looked down at the red and black scars running down the length of my arm. I grabbed the butterfly needle out of her hand, stuck it once and blood flowed out of the tube in spurts. She grabbed the vacuum test tube, plugged it in, and collected her sample. This is where a lot of other prisoners had to toughen up, because believe me, being scared of needles is not some girl thing. There were guys passing out, freaking out and crying like babies. They all had their turn and fear of pain is not something you want people in jail to see. Through muffled cries and hidden tears, they silently went through their own hell.

Finally my name was called and I was led up to psych. There were only about ten other guys going up to the psych ward with me, so I said goodbye to my friends going into population and shuffled through another series of stairs and concrete. We got to our cell block, grabbed a mattress, and were assigned our bunks.

As soon as we walked into the block, a few of the crazies started hammering on the plexiglass doors of their solitary cells, making slashing motions across their throats and pointing out the ones they wanted to kill. Each block had about twenty solitary cells, twenty double bunk cells and twelve double beds in a common area for eating. I was thrilled when they called my cell number and it was on the upper berth- a solitary cell. At least for three days I would be safe and alone and could go through my detox in peace. My electronic door clicked open, I threw my mattress on the steel slab, wrapped my torn up white sheet around it, wound up in a little ball and fell asleep for ten or twenty minutes.

The next three days were uneventful. I lay in bed, sleepless, the large fluorescent light over my head never turning off, and thought about my first hit of dope when I got out. I was counting the minutes until my release. The truth was I had no idea when I was getting out. I had been arrested making a deal on the street, so I had a narcotics investigation charge pending. I've seen guys get three years for that. All I could do was hope for the best and pray I could work my magic on the judge.

The psychotics weren't allowed to mix with the rest of the block at any time and there were one or two guys from the street I knew in here. It was also twenty-four-hour suicide watch, so the guards had a tower watching five other blocks arranged in a semicircle with ours. I dreaded going into population. There were people getting killed in the riots. The County Jail made the front page of the L.A. Times during that time because of the violence and injuries.

On the third day of my stay in the luxury solo suite of the psycho ward I was called out to see the doctor. I still had to sit patiently in a hallway on a hard metal bench for three hours before going in, but I was hoping to get doped up at the end of it. No such luck. The doctor asked what was the matter? I told him I was going through withdrawal and anything he could give me would be much appreciated. He asked if I had any thoughts of suicide, any allergies, or took any regular medication. I said yeah, Colonopin for anxiety, and Xanex for sleeplessness.

He asked me my dosage and the amount I told him was about five hundred milligrams higher than the dosage allowed by law, so he knew I was just trying to score some heavy meds from him. He gave me two aspirin and some medicine for diarrhea, neither of which worked, and signed me out. This was good because I was one step closer to hopefully being released and I prayed I could see the judge the next morning. It was Thursday night, and if I couldn't see her the next day I would be in all weekend again.

After another six hours of waiting around, they called my name so I could be transferred into the main dormitories. I handed in my raggedy mattress and blanket and marched through a period of another six hours from cell to cell. We wound up in a long hallway that went under the street and into the belly of the old L.A. county jail.

The one I had just left was called the glass house. It was fairly modern, as much as a building of concrete, jail bars, and plexiglass could be. The one I walked into, the old county jail, was a nightmare. Toilets were backed up, big chunks of lead paint chipped off of the crumbling walls and you could only see sunlight through a cell that was far down the hall. It was a dark and depressing place, and the mood in there was either aggressive or somber. The smell and whispers of murders that had taken place in those cells were always present. I was led up the stairs to my dorm, given the filthiest, most stained mattress I had ever seen in my life, told I would be given a bed assignment by the guard and thrown into the jungle.

CHAPTER SIX

Not having a bunk assignment, I went to a table with a checkerboard on it in the middle of the room, sat my ass down, and collapsed my head into my arms. After a few minutes I felt someone breathing down my neck and looked up to see about five huge guys surrounding me.

"You can't sit here"

"I don't have a bunk yet."

"That's your problem."

Luckily, I was rescued.

"Hold it, hold it, he's with me. C'mon, I'll get you a bunk. I'm Rob, the wood rep. I'll show you around."

Telling me he was the wood rep meant he was going make sure I stayed out of trouble. White people are called 'woods', short for 'peckerwoods'. The white of fers will say "WOOD!" to get your attention, so everyone just calls white guys wood. It's just the way things are, the same way a black guy might be called "BLACK" or "LIGHT SKIN" or another term that focuses on your skin color. All of the prisoners are divided by race. It is not a choice there is to make.

Despite the micro political system they had set up here, this was the worst time for me to be in. The black and Mexican gangs were at war and riots had been breaking out for the last four days. We heard about them in the psych ward and we knew that people were getting knifed and severely beaten. There was no question where I was expected to stand, but I had no desire to get into a war that I wasn't a part of.

I had never been exposed to racism as a kid. I lived in a very unique neighborhood in rural Michigan. My father was a chemical engineer at Dow, who had a very liberal hiring policy because of the Vietnam War. A large percentage of graduate age men had been drafted and so Dow hired outside of the norm, bringing in chemists from all over the world based on their qualifications rather than their place of birth or skin color. Since they were all paid relatively the same, we all lived in nice houses with woods all around and plenty of space. The kids in my neighborhood were African American, East Indian, Jewish, Chinese, Potowomac Indian, Muslim, Columbian, English, Japanese, Mexican, Persian, and on and on.

There were several new year's eve parties throughout the year as different religions hit theirs. Our birthday parties were cross cultural events with treats from all over the world. My favorites were the Sikh (East Indian) mothers. One family had perhaps twelve members living under one roof and they all wore these beautiful bright sarongs and always smiled and fed us and I loved them. At eleven years old I learned about the Indian Caste system and the oppression of slaves worldwide and how people are judged by skin color. It made no sense to me because I formed attachments to children of all races before I had the chance to surround myself with only white friends and only white ideologies. Even today I see white friends who had the opposite happen in their lives and were only surrounded by white kids then, and guess what... they're only surrounded by white people now.

I ran into one of my buddies from the street, a Latino who called himself Spider. I loved how these guys talked and never hesitated to pick up their speech.

"Heeeeyyy, wasssup, homie? Welcome to paradise haha! How you been? When did you get in?" He spoke to me like an old friend and I breathed a sigh of relief.

"Six days ago. I had to go through psych ward in the glass house. How long you been here?"

"Two weeks, man, I got parole violation. You kicking dope?"

"Yeah, it sucks, the doctor didn't do shit. I'm hoping to go to court in the morning."

"Probably won't happen if you just got here today. Also, someone might target you to get you in a drug debt, DO

NOT DO IT, you might want the hit now, but your butthole is gonna pay later HAHA! You hear about what's happening?"

He proceeded to tell me territory wars over drugs in the street had spilled into the jail, and leaders of the black gangs and the Mexican mafia had given a green light to attack on sight any rival gang member. Younger members on both sides were eager to get respect from the higher ups and they knew the more aggressive and violent they were the more they would get noticed. This was all happening right here, right now, in the very room I was in. It happens every day on the street too but I had walked into a concentrated ball of gang racism and hatred, and it permeated the air everywhere.

CHAPTER SEVEN

Every morning at three thirty A.M. just after breakfast the dorm reps would be handed sheets of paper with assignments for inmates to go to court. They had the bed numbers on them so no names were read off, they just walked down the isles handing out the pieces of paper to whoever got to see the judge that day. I had been expecting one since I first walked in there but so was everyone else. It was a tightrope because you could get released right from the courtroom or you could be given a continuance and that could take weeks or even months before you actually had your trial. After that you could STILL be given more time depending on your crime and previous record.

I tried to psych myself out with logic. I had a pending narcotics investigation with "suspicion of being under the influence of a controlled substance". This wasn't possession, this wasn't trafficking nor intent to sell or suspicion of being under the influence of a controlled substance. The last one was a bullshit charge. EVERYONE is under suspicion of being under the influence. It was what they charged people with when they wanted to put them away but didn't have any evidence to plant.

There are two ways they do this, one of which is "suspicion of being under the influence", a very popular charge in Los Angeles.

Suspicion? How can you charge someone with 'suspicion'?

Aren't you supposed to charge people with, "Positive, no question, he did this because I saw it or I have witnesses"?

Suspicion means that any cop, at any time, for any reason, can charge a person with suspicion of being under the influence without giving them any kind of test to see whether or not they are actually under the influence. The test is administered later in the jail, and the presumed guilty party is already in custody.

People who are heroin addicts are easy targets because they need to get outside of the jail to score dope and they'll say or do anything to get it.

The lawyer walks up to you and says, "You want to get out of here today? You have a narcotics investigation pending. If you plead guilty, I can get you released today. If you plead not guilty you may not be released and may have to wait for a hearing If the judge wants to drag out your case or actually open the narcotics investigation you can be here for several months if they do not want to release you, which they can do at their discretion."

These cops weren't going to waste any time on an investigation of a small-time street deal. I made a hundred mental notes on what I could tell the judge- Whether I got a court date, sentenced, or released, at least I would know. The hardest part of being in jail is not knowing when you'll get out.

Finally, my day came. The wood rep got up to get the court sheets, and before I knew it I had one in my hand. Everyone going to court got all excited and I was counting the hours until my first hit. I tried to think positive, no reassigned court date, no extended sentence, just time served and get the fuck out of my jail. The announcement came for all going to court to get in line, so we shook hands, hugged our jealous friends and lined up like little blue soldiers.

Over three hours they counted us, I.D. ed us, chained us up and threw us on a bus. They had the radio on again but we were too excited to sing. We talked to each other about our charges and a lot of the guys had been busted so many times they knew exactly what state statutes would apply in the hearing, and would often argue with their state's attorney before the hearing about which motions to file.

After a fifty-minute drive and another two hours of holding cells we were ushered into the courtroom behind a plexiglass wall. It wasn't looking good. The first guy we saw when we walked in turned and said, "Man, this chick is a BITCH!" He went on to tell us all of the previous cases had gotten harsh sentences or delayed hearings, keeping guys with minimal charges and maximum families in for an extended stay.

No one was getting released. Most of the guys in there were expecting to be let out and they all got future court dates, which means if no one bails you out you're in here for a while. The judge definitely had a chip on her shoulder. Ohhh, this did not look good.

As I waited for my name to be called, I was almost in tears. I was raised in a decent Michigan town, and had fulfilled a lifelong dream of getting a record contract in Hollywood and played shows all over the world. How the fuck did I wind up a homeless dope addict within three years? How did I get mixed up with an L.A. gang and talk them into letting me sell smack on the street for them? How was I going to clean up the mess my life had become?

We called ourselves 'lifers' because we believed

we would die as addicts.

CHAPTER EIGHT-

Two years earlier

Going right from the Hawaiian Islands to downtown L.A. was a little harsh. The flowering trees and exotic birds had been replaced by graffiti covered buildings and homeless crack addicts. But the city was raw and alive, the dope cheap and plentiful, and danger lurked in every alleyway. I had missed it.

I found an apartment on the southern boardwalk of Venice Beach in a little town called Marina Del Rey. It was a bit smoother of a transition between Hawaii and Hollywood, right on the beach, but only a forty-minute bus ride from downtown Los Angeles. Venice was the perfect location for me. My front steps opened up on the famous boardwalk, and I fit right in. Everywhere you look in Venice has been a backdrop for a movie or television show and the standard mode of transportation is skateboarding.

Having been a skateboarder since early childhood, I bought a new board and skated the entire boardwalk back and forth every morning. I hung out with the hippies and smoked legal medical chronic herb and tanned while drinking draft beers in outdoor cafes while talking to my friends freezing their asses off in Chicago or New York. On Sundays there was a drum circle on the beach, and we danced till well after sunset with Hare Krishnas in their flowing robes and Rastafarians that desperately needed a bath. I often sat out on the boardwalk with my guitar and belted out some delta blues for tourists and bikini clad college girls.

I started calling all of my old business contacts. I used to make a good living selling music to television shows, video game companies, movie music coordinators, and had an extremely impressive resume of five-star clients. I had an appearance in the first ever streaming music video in a game and was just one of the hundreds of credits I had. I thought it would be easy to jump right back in, put together a press kit with a few cd's to send out to agents and music directors and the clients would come knocking.

I figured I had enough money to last me for about four months, so I paid my rent as far in advance as I could. This was always a good idea because you would be in good with the landlord and he wouldn't jump down your throat if you were late with the rent later on but also because you wouldn't spend the money on anything else. There was only one anything else I had, and the balloons I was picking up from downtown were lasting for shorter and shorter amounts of time.

Addiction is a progressive disease, so you don't jump into it right away. You find excuses to do it then it gets to a point where you don't even need an excuse anymore. The dope was so much cheaper in Los Angeles ($5 a bag compared to $20 in Hawaii) I figured I could easily afford a habit. This might have been true if I had money coming in, but I was spending the money I had saved and between the expensive apartment on the beach and a sixty dollar a day habit I was quickly running out of cash and running out of options.

I tried putting the dope habit down. Heroin addiction is like no other addiction in that you experience a very painful withdrawal when you don't have it. I wasn't so far gone in my addiction that I couldn't have quit and gone through more than a week of the flu like symptoms, but the psychological part had hold of me as well. I wasn't getting any responses from the music I was sending out for licensing and I didn't want to get a nine to five job. It only took one licensing contract to keep me afloat because they usually paid really well, upwards of $7,000 to $20,000 per commercial or film.

A video game soundtrack license would pay between five and ten thousand dollars, and a television show might pay twelve hundred to five thousand depending on the show but it also paid royalties through ASCAP every time the show was aired. I had hundreds of these types of credits and every quarter I was issued a check for a decent amount from licensing royalties. This wasn't enough to last very long and it would be a while before I got my next check. A movie soundtrack could pay up to fifty thousand dollars, but from the time the initial request was made to the time payment was made (usually after the release of the film) it could be six months to a year. I was starting to get desperate.

The first thing I did was to get rid of my apartment. Two thousand a month to live on the beach was a luxury, not a necessity. I found a friend who was looking for a roommate, and I thought seven hundred (my half) was something I could easily afford. My landlord was nice enough to give me my deposit back, so I had enough for another few months. I went out looking for a job and was lucky to find something right away that suited me. I had applied at and was accepted for employment at one of Hollywood's big music stores selling pro audio gear.

Every morning I took the train down to the city to score dope on 5th and Broadway, then hustled back up to go to work. I usually got there on time, but sometimes there was no dope to be found. I would show up on Broadway at eight o'clock, an hour before work and there would be fifty to a hundred junkies walking in circles around the block. I started to get to know a lot of them and usually someone from the drug dealing gangs was there to tell everyone it would only be another half an hour. If he wasn't there everyone would walk six blocks to the other spot, sixth and Gladys, in the middle of Skid Row.

Once you passed Los Angeles boulevard, three blocks away from Broadway, you entered what you can tell is a world unlike the rest of the city. Really it's unlike the rest of the planet. Men walked around in shabby winter coats in the middle of summer, doing their best to keep the chills of heroin withdrawal to a minimum. Tents were lined up along the sidewalk with the residents sitting nearby cooking food or drinking beer. The amount of rotting trash on the streets and sidewalks increased daily.

There was usually a crowd around one part of the street, someone serving food, or giving out soap and if there was a line, people usually just stepped into it without asking what they were in line for, knowing it would be food or supplies.

In the center of Skid Row were the missions, The Midnight, The Union, and several other smaller ones. There was always a crowd outside of the entrances as workers and volunteers stepped outside for a cigarette or people lined up to get a meal or a bed. The poor look the same today as they always have. Bereft of friends and family to keep them up in appearances, not having a significant other, employment, or children nearby to need to be pressed and cleaned for, not having a safe place to wash and keep clean clothes, the level of untidiness goes from not at all to severely unhealthy.

Their disarray starts at shirts being untucked and shoes being untied to people dressed in hospital gowns, their skin blackened from lack of showering and their ass hanging out the always untied back. The mentally disabled are always in the worst shape, clothes stained black from top to bottom from the inability to properly clean themselves, their hair all disheveled and often containing insect nests. Mites, bedbugs, and especially body lice are always spread throughout the entire district and no matter how clean a spot gets, within a few days it has an infestation to deal with. Most of them are simply dealt with on a day to day basis as spending the time and money to eradicate them completely will be wasted as the next day someone will have brought the bugs back to contaminate the area again.

Some of the mentally disabled have had bugs nest in their hair so thick that the top of their head looks like one moving shadow. If you get closer you find that ten thousand little lice bugs are swarming on the head of a human being. People like this are quickly picked up by social services and usually never seen again. A person who poses a health risk to the others in the community is quickly ostracized, as body lice and tuberculosis, STAPH and hepatitis are looked for by the other residents, and people with even slight symptoms are pushed away from the others.

The shops that are open are almost exclusively for Skid Row residents and usually serve cigarettes, crack pipes and high sugar items like ice cream bars and chocolate or junk food (burgers or fried chicken, mashed potatoes, etc.) There are no liquor stores for about three blocks in any direction but no one seems to mind the ten minutes it takes to get there. There's also a marijuana dispensary that sells big bags of chronic shake for $10, and it tasted like pesticides burning in your throat.

A bit further west there's a few drug stores and you get into more of a shopping district and commuter hub on Broadway and Fifth. Further south on San Pedro is a warehouse district with art supply stores, the flower district, and if you keep going you run into Santee Alley, a street for pedestrians only and lined with as many little shops as a Turkish bazaar. From the East, it's mostly frozen fish warehouses, a few scattered factories, some good clothing stores, and that bridge you see in every movie filmed in Los Angeles.

I was dressed up for work in pressed black suit pants and a nice collared shirt, looking completely out of place. I would later learn that carrying a clipboard or having a plastic volunteer tag made you invisible to all no matter how you dressed. The volunteers came down here in droves and they had a special pass from the Skid Row residents to go about their business without being hindered or asked for cash, and are easily identifiable by ubiquitous clipboards, plastic laminate name tags, and permanent nervous smiles. In the meantime I was very obvious and stood out like a sore thumb. Standing out is not such a good thing on Skid Row. Everyone knows you're buying dope, and buyers are targeted by junkies desperate for a fix.

If nobody showed up with any dope by eight thirty I would start to panic. My job started a meeting for everyone on the shift at nine o'clock ON THE NOSE and if you were even one minute late everyone turned and looked at you. I had to make a choice at about eight thirty; stay here an extra ten minutes and pray someone would show up with dope, run down to Skid Row and try to score there, or go to work and be dope sick all day.

The worst was when someone actually did show up on Broadway. With fifty junkies there, all of them sick, if only one dealer showed up he was MOBBED by junkies sticking money in his face trying to get their dope to get well. Often the dealers got spooked and ran because as much as they screamed "BACK OFF ME!!", junkies were nearly assaulting them, trying to get their hands on what little dope there was. If you didn't get in there quick you were shit out of luck and had to wait for the next dealer to show up but that could take hours.

I had gotten to a point of desperation. I had my check for two weeks' work and was totally out of options. I had crashed on as many friends' couches for as long as I could but that had run its course. I could've paid my hotel for the next two weeks but then I would've been broke and would have to scramble downtown every morning with ten or twenty dollars I made the night before playing guitar on Hollywood boulevard. In order to keep my job, I would have to buy enough dope so I would not have to go downtown every morning and to do that I would have to keep the money I was going to use for my hotel. I picked up my things from the room I was paying for, threw the excess in a storage space I was renting for a hundred bucks a month, and moved into my car.

It was actually really comfortable. Chevy Blazers are spacious machines, and mine was a 95 so it wasn't as huge as those old boats from the eighties but I could flip the back seat down and spread a blanket in the back and have room to stretch out. I bought a few packs of dope for a hundred dollars and settled in. Each pack held twelve balloons and each balloon was one hit. This was around 2004, so the dope in the balloons from the gangs on Broadway was quality and decent sized. It would only take one balloon in the morning to cure the sickness, but I usually did two- one to get well, one to get high.

I took one with me to do at lunchtime at work, and when I got home to the car, I did one or two and then one or two to go to bed. A pack usually lasted me two days at fifty dollars a pack, so it cost me about seven hundred dollars every two weeks to support my habit. My check from work was about nine hundred every two weeks, figure in food and gas and I was right about on the money.

For a few weeks it seemed like I could hold out like that. I would get my paycheck, buy two packs at a time and try to make it hold out as long as possible. I had to move my car around to different spots to avoid detection or getting towed when the street sweepers came, but I always read the signs to know when that would be. I stayed on the west side of Hollywood close to work, so I usually walked from where I was parked every morning.

I had it down to a routine. I'd wash my clothes every few days at a Laundromat so I had fresh digs and I kept a gallon jug of water in the car so I could take a quick birdbath in the morning and wash my hair. I had cut out some cardboard boxes to fit in my windows and block out the sun or to keep people from seeing inside, and I had a purple velvet curtain behind the front seat that blocked the view of everything behind it.

I had a few nice big blankets in the back, one to lay down on and one to cover myself with. With a candle or two lit it stayed nice and toasty in there and I could crack the rear window to ventilate the smoke when I wanted a cigarette. I had my cell phone working, so communication with the outside world was possible and I kept praying for just ONE licensing gig so I could get an apartment or at least move back into the hotels. I washed clothes at the local laundromat and I peed in water bottles I kept in plentiful supply. Keep your city clean.

I was moving some things into my storage space on Hollywood Boulevard, and had the Blazer packed full. I stopped at the El Pollo Loco on Western and Hollywood to grab a bite to eat, and upon leaving the restaurant jumped in the driver's seat and pulled out my works to take a little after dinner hit. Heroin feels good on a full stomach. It curbs your appetite so if you hit before eating, you won't eat. It was twilight and a cool breeze blew through the city in an almost glamorous way that mixes with your high to make an after-dinner cigarette in a parking lot feel like a 70's album cover.

CHAPTER NINE

I sat in the car for twenty minutes, enjoying my high and letting the cool air relax me to a state of almost sleep. I decided to get moving and stash my things before the storage closed otherwise I'd be cramped in the rear cab with all of my records and framed pictures for the night. I started the car up and to this day I am so thankful I was facing the rear brick wall and not the restaurant. A two by four piece of wood had jammed under the brake and across the accelerator, and when I pulled the shifter into drive and tapped on the brake, the car lurched forward. I panicked, jammed my foot on the brake, but the wood kept the brake from pressing down and it hit the accelerator full on.

In a split second the car jumped up to thirty miles an hour in about four yards of space.

I had a split second to swerve around a car parked in a stall, and then hit the brick wall at full force.

I woke up about thirty seconds later. Steam was rising out of the smashed-in front end of my car and blood was spewing down my face from where I hit the steering wheel with the bridge of my nose. There were twenty people standing around me, others running to get towels for my face and talking to me in Spanish. I had NO idea what had just happened. I hadn't hit anything besides the cinder block wall, which was now boasting a hole the size of my engine. I looked into the passenger seat and gathered up my needles and cooker because the cops were SURE to come and stashed them all in my hiding spot under the safety brake.

After taking a few minutes to get my bearings, I cleaned up my face with water and towels someone had brought me and looked at the damage.

My front end was totaled. The radiator was crushed and the fluid from it was now all over the parking lot. Fuck. My mobile home was now an accordion. Chevy trucks are built like tanks and this being my third one, I didn't hesitate to turn over the ignition and it started right up! I put it in reverse, backed over the curb and out of the hole in the wall, and aside from LOOKING like I had just run it into a brick wall, it ran fine!

I knew the engine would overheat with no fluid in the radiator so I turned it off and sat talking to the guy who was the property manager. He wanted to fill out a police report but I knew it would be hours before the cops showed up on a non-emergency call, so I pulled out of the lot and with my front bumper hanging on by a thread, made it to my storage space before they closed.

Within a week my face was healed, and aside from having to carry around gallons of water and radiator fluid to keep from overheating, things went back to normal. For a heroin addict, normal means things are burning down around you and you don't care.

I was hanging on by my fingernails, but at least I was hanging on, then the worst thing that could happen, did. My car was parked just north of Melrose Avenue near a friend's house who was letting me shower. I had already gotten a few parking tickets from moving my car around but had no money to pay for them so I just blew them off. Sure enough, I came home to find the Department of Motor Vehicles had left me a little present. There on my car, along with a bright orange ticket, was a Denver boot.

FUCK! I knew this was bad. I called the number on the ticket and to pay off all of the violations I had (which were doubled once you had a boot on) PLUS the fine to remove the boot would be around eighteen hundred bucks. Shit, the car only cost me about two grand, but it was my home. I scrambled around to see if I could borrow from anyone, but that kind of money was just not available. I even thought about getting a hacksaw and removing the damn thing myself, but then I would be criminally liable and I didn't want to go to jail. I figured I had about four or five days until they towed me then I would be out on the street.

I went to bed in my car that night, snug and warm and trying not to think about how horrible my life was about to become. I did the last few hits of dope I had stashed and fell into a blissful slumber. The next morning I woke up not really dope sick but feeling the craving. I went to work as usual and knew about halfway through the day I was fucked. I was starting to get stomach cramps, blurred vision, and sweats to the point where people were asking me, "Are you okay?"

As soon as my shift ended I was on the bus towards the red line to go downtown. I figured instead of going cold turkey I could just gradually decline my use and be okay. This is a lie we addicts tell ourselves over and over and over again. William Burroughs even had a word for it, he called it a "Chinese detox". According to Mr. Burroughs, take and cook up the last of your dope, making sure there's enough for a few days. Every time you do a hit, you squirt the same amount of water into the vial. The junk gets more and more diluted, and it didn't work for me in the least.

I got off the red line at Pershing Square, started the junkie walk around Broadway to find a dealer and finally scored. I only grabbed one balloon, but one was enough. I took the train all the way back to Hollywood, hopped on the bus to Melrose where my car was parked, got into the back seat, undressed, and lit a few candles. I set out my works, water, and needle, and opened up my balloon to put me to sleep. I opened it up, and almost cried. It was a cigarette butt. I had been scammed.

I couldn't sleep that night. Sleeplessness is one of the tortures of withdrawal along with the other sicknesses that comes with it. It was too late to go back. Nobody would be around. They stop selling at around seven o'clock and I would have to wait until morning. The thing about Heroin is it makes you forget how bad things actually are. You feel like you can handle anything, no matter how bad it gets. When you're in withdrawal it amplifies your feelings of fear, hopelessness, and dread. It makes you think about suicide. Paranoia runs deep as well and I was sure they were coming to tow my car that night. Every car that drove by made me shiver, and I lay awake looking at the roof and counting the minutes until morning.

Finally, the time came. It was about six A.M., and the dealers would be out on the street. I jumped out of the car, no birdbath, no shower, no clean clothes, and headed downtown. It didn't take me long to find a dealer, and I scored four balloons. I had plenty of time before work, so I sat outside the train station and had a cigarette before jumping back on.

"Would you step over here please?"

It was two L.A. sheriff's deputies in a patrol car. They were not an uncommon sight near the red line station in the morning, but they usually just checked people for tickets and kept homeless people from panhandling passengers.

"Yeah, sure what's the problem, officer?"

I was trying to be polite. Sometimes they just asked you a few questions and let you go. I was dressed in my work clothes, so I didn't think I was under suspicion.

"You know it's illegal to smoke here?"

"No, I wasn't on the train. I was having a cigarette before I went to work."

He was already getting the cuffs out.

"This is Metro property. You're not allowed to smoke here"

Oh. Shit.

"What are you doing down here anyway?"

"I was just having breakfast at my favorite spot. You know, that restaurant over there on fifth? They got the best breakfast for four bucks. Ham and eggs, pancakes, sausages, orange juice, the works. You ever eat there?"

I was trying to distract them. I had the balloons in my pocket and if I got searched I knew they would be found.

"Yeah, why don't you step over here by the car and place your hands on the hood."

FUCK! I was in big trouble. All I could do was hope they didn't find them but I was shaking. They handcuffed me, lifted my shirt sleeves, and saw the red and black track marks running down my arm.

"Weeeeellllllll, look what we got here. You got any dope on you?"

"No, sir."

I wasn't going to make their job any EASIER for them. They started going through my stuff and spreading it out on the hood. Keys, wallet, train pass, work pass, and.....

"What's this?? Looks like you got one, two, three, four balloons here. When's the last time you were arrested?"

"I've never been arrested, sir, and I have a job. If you arrest me now, I'm going to lose my job, and you'll have one more homeless guy out on the streets here. Can't you cut me a break?"

He went to converse with his partner for a few minutes while they were waiting for my record to come back. Sure enough, clean as a whistle, and they debated for a few minutes on what to do.

"Well buddy, we're going to give you a choice. You can either go to jail, or you can make a buy for us. We'll be watching you from the building across the street, so whoever you buy from won't know it's you that got 'em busted, and you can go home."

For some reason all I kept thinking was that it was getting late, and I HATED being late for work.

"Man, if I do that, then these guys will KILL me. Not figuratively, LITERALLY. If I do that, I'm a dead man."

"Well. Your other choice is to go to jail. LITERALLY."

I knew I had no choice. I started down the block, giving them five minutes to get into position across the street. I STILL felt like I was getting set up. I figured there were video cameras and other detectives who would be witnesses to the buy, and there was NO WAY they would just take the dope I bought as evidence and let me go on my merry way. I had to go along with what they said and turned the corner on to Broadway.

The gangsters were everywhere and every one of them I passed was asking me if I wanted heroin. I remember looking at the faces wondering whose life I was about to ruin.

It was a shitty feeling.

I'm no snitch, but my back was against the wall and I thought hard for a way out of this. I was thinking about running but the cops already had my I.D. and they would just put out a warrant for me. If I went THROUGH with this, I would be marked by the 5th and Hill gang as a snitch and probably stabbed as I went to score at some point in the future. I saw a bunch of youngsters peddling dope and I thought man, I don't want to ruin the life of some kid that young. I mean, it's their choice and they know the consequences of what they are doing, but it would suck to see some kid that young go down because of me. These older guys all already have records.

It was a tough spot and as I walked down the block I was starting to sweat.

Down at the end of the street, I saw the perfect candidate.

It was the guy who ripped me off last night. Had he sold me real dope I would not even consider it because then I would be able to score from him in the future, but there he was, selling to a group of kids that couldn't have been more than fifteen. I knew he wasn't a gang banger. He was just some junkie trying to make his own fix by selling for the gang.

I walked right up to him, hoping he wouldn't recognize me from last night and sure enough he didn't.

"Gimme four" I said and threw twenty dollars at him. I knew he wouldn't be selling fake shit in the morning, there were too many people around and he would get jumped for ripping people off. I walked back around the corner, gave the cops one of them and kept the other three in my mouth. Sure enough, they were good to their word. I thought they might keep me to act as a witness or something but I was released. I walked down the other side of the street to watch the action and within three minutes another patrol car screeched up alongside theirs and rolled right up on him. I saw him turn and walk away from the middle of a sale but they were all over him. He was screaming, "WHAT?!? WHAT?!?!" as they shoved him into the car and sped off. The whole thing took less than a minute. I didn't feel bad about it at all.

I jumped on the train and sped off to work. I knew if I didn't fix here I would have to sit through a half hour meeting at work and then try to do it in the bathroom when the store was opening, which was the worst time to be missing. It's not a real smart thing to fix on the train either because they have undercover cops working the red line, but I was sick and desperate.

I rolled up into a little ball in one of the rear seats, cooked up the dope in a plastic tin I had with me, took off one of my shoes, and hit a vein in my foot.

All of the stress of the last few days melted away.

My life was falling down around me and I didn't care.

I was invincible once again.

I didn't care about anything or anyone, myself especially.

That's why people love dope so much. No matter how bad things are, if you're high, you really don't care as they continue to get worse.

I had the next day off and so I stayed by the car. There was street sweeping that day and I didn't want to get towed earlier than I was going to be anyway, so I sat and waited for the tow truck to come. When they showed up I explained that my car was booted, but someone was going to pay the tickets right now and they would remove the boot. They said fine, whatever, and let me be. I had lucked out for the moment, but I knew the day was coming soon and I was totally out of options.

I was really pretty comfortable in my car. The people in the neighborhood were starting to eye me in a peculiar way. I guess I would have too, here was this guy washing his hair out the passenger side rear door, brushing his teeth with water bottles and who knows what else, but nobody was calling the cops just yet. I had a storage space in Hollywood so anything valuable was already put away. I was sleeping really well, the noise of outside traffic just lulled me to rest and I felt safe and secure.

CHAPTER TEN

Eventually the day came. It took about ten days after I was first booted. I was beginning to think they forgot about me but that was just wishful thinking. I came home from work one day and walked down the beautiful, tree- lined yuppie apartment street I was parked on, and it was just gone. There was another car in the spot where I had been, and it was just gone. I sat and put my head between my knees. All of my clothes, my needles, anything I needed for day to day use was gone as well. I knew this day was approaching and tried to plan ahead, but there was just nothing I could do. I tried to quit dope but failed. I called a friend and told him I was fucked for the night and asked if I could crash. He was a good friend and one I didn't want to take advantage of but this was a tight spot.

The next day at work I told a friend a little about my plight and he told me I could crash at his place. Okay, so I've got a place tonight. It doesn't make things much better, but at least I'm okay tonight. We got off of work and he told me to come by around ten o'clock. I went by my other friend's place and grabbed the few things I had and watched t.v. for a few minutes.

At nine-thirty I head out towards my other friend's place and called to make sure he was home. No answer. I waited twenty minutes and called again. Still no answer. I walked up to where he lived near Hollywood and Highland, figuring he was just out and I wanted to be nearby when he got home. It was freezing out, not the sub-zero cold they get in the north, but a little above forty degrees, which is freezing for Hollywood and VERY uncomfortable to be outside for the night.

Finally, at eleven o clock I got hold of him.

"Hey, man listen, I'm really sorry, but my roommate's being kind of weird. He doesn't know you or anything and he doesn't want me having any guests. I'm really sorry."

"WHAT?! Listen, man, I hear what you're saying, but it's eleven o' clock at night. I can't start calling around looking for a place to stay NOW! It's freezing outside! Look, just tell him I'll crash on the floor or whatever and be gone first thing in the morning!! Look, you can't back out on me at the last minute like this! PLEASE!"

"Yeah, I'm sorry, but he's pretty much got the say on what goes on around here. His folks paid the deposit and if he says something I gotta go with it."

"Look, I understand, but I'm really fucked! It's too late at night to call anyone else! If you would've told me earlier I would've found another place but it's late and it's COLD and you can't back out on me now!!"

"I'm sorry man but I just can't do it. Maybe next week."

I started to realize what a bad situation I was actually in. I had nowhere to go and it was too late to start making calls to impose on any friends I had left. I was at the mall on Hollywood and Highland in the Kodak Oscar Museum. It was late and they were starting to close. I sat in the rest room in one of the stalls to keep warm. The Oscar Museum is an outdoor mall, so standing outside I was getting chilly, and I had nowhere to go. I sat in the rest room in one of the stalls to keep warm.

There's a weird feeling you get when you realize for the first time that you have absolutely nowhere to go. There is no one waiting for you, there is no bed with your name on it, no one is going to check to see if you have eaten, no one is expecting you or hoping that you'll call. There's nowhere for you to comfortably go to the bathroom, no place for you to put your clothes, no rows of socks in dresser drawers, no safe place to keep your best photographs, no bed to make, no shoes to shine, no toothbrush in the holder under the mirror, nothing. You have pretty much what you are carrying and you had better make the best of it. Too much stuff, and you'll be weighed down. Not enough, and you might be missing something crucial; you need wet weather gear, toiletries, at least one change of clothes, extra food, blanket, sleeping roll, wallet, the number of things that you should carry with you to stay healthy, safe, warm, and clean is too much for any one person to carry and there are entire families who push shopping carts filled with their treasures all over Skid Row.

You look at the world in a whole new way. There's nowhere you belong. There's nowhere you can clean up, make something to eat, or even sit down in a comfortable way. You're homeless. The world is your bedroom, the grass and sidewalks are your bed. It's a very unsettling feeling, and one I will never forget. There's no money coming in. There's no relative you can call to stay with them. You're just out on your own and nobody cares. The last person who cared tossed you out when they found a needle and cried when they did it.

Soon a security guard came in.

BAM! BAM! "We're closing up, sir, you need to vacate the premises!"

"Yeah, okay, I'll be out in a minute."

I stepped outside and looked around. I took the escalator downstairs and noticed there were a few of those portable kiosks on wheels parked in a corner behind the escalator. I sat down behind them where no one could see me, put my head in between my knees and started to cry. I was getting dope sick as well and the chilly air was making me shake. At least the kiosks were blocking the wind a little bit. I was out of sight but I knew if they caught me there after hours I would be thrown out or arrested.

An announcement came over the loudspeaker system that the mall would be closing in five minutes. I had no choice but to walk the streets and hope to find somewhere to curl up out of the cold. This is what true despair feels like.

CHAPTER ELEVEN

They say that young girls are a sign of a healthy community. When an area starts to decay, the first thing to go are the young women. As an army approaches or new buildings turn to old, the young and beautiful women of the community are kept closest to the epicenter of wealth and status, the safest level of the castle, or snuck out the back to a mountain hideaway with an easily defendable single trail passage where invading soldiers could be picked off one by one. This makes the fighting especially intense and can be the determining factor when rallying the troops.

I think all women are beautiful and there certainly are appearances of some striking girls down on Skid Row, but never for very long. The relentless and ubiquitous requests for sex, paid and free, force women to look for a room elsewhere. I despair thinking about what happens to even younger and more beautiful girls I've seen walking around Skid Row, desperate looks on their faces as they talk with a boyfriend or one of the locals. Soon their faces are gone. I hate to think of where. It's usually within a day or two.

The boyfriend can be seen endlessly circling the streets, looking in vain for his woman, the woman he promised to take care of, and now she's missing. He fills out the police reports, he puts up the flyers, but the fact of the matter is that she might never be found. Pretty young women who come to Skid Row are targeted the minute they step foot off of the bus, sometimes sooner. Women who are unable to provide are pretty much left to fend for themselves on the street.

This means that Skid Row is partially populated with the women of the Los Angeles area whom no one wants to take care of, thrown out by relatives, no longer able to make good money for pimps, not able to be employed, and most are dead broke. They perform sex acts on the homeless for a pittance. Usually as little as some change or a few little crumbs of crack are enough to obtain the services of many of the women when nights are slow.

The competition for attention from cars is fierce. Competing pimps get to draw out their corners, often allowing women to swap if one corner is hot or all of his women are out. The girls dance endlessly around the four sidewalk corners, looking as if they could say, "Hey I'm just waiting for a bus officer", and gossip into the night.

I once spent three nights with a girl who asked me to stay with her while she was working. It's not uncommon for the girls to ask this of a friend, mostly so the tricks see there is someone with the girl who can identify them or their car if necessary. The girls are also targeted by other pimps who will use the girl and take back the money or beat her in order to see what the first pimp will do, if he will defend his territory violently or if he'll just let the girl go to avoid bloodshed. Blood and bullets mean police, and police mean business has to stop until the issue is resolved.

She wanted me to stand on the corner close to her while she approached the cars and made the deals. This little bit of insurance was a good score for me. She had a tent close by and within the hour she had enough dope for me to stay happy while she turned her tricks. She was always coming back to the tent to take a few hits of crack before walking back out into the night where the next guy was already waiting. This went on all night and into the early hours of the morning.

I kept talking to the other girls while my girl was gone and some of them asked if I would do the same for them. I was only too happy to walk each and every one of them who requested a safe walk to the car they got into and made a show out of checking the looks of the driver and the license number. Often, they'd be back in forty minutes with three hundred dollars. Just as often the three hundred was gone within thirty minutes.

CHAPTER TWELVE

I was still in the kiosks at the Hollywood and Highland Oscar Museum and they were closing up. As I got up to leave, I noticed a rectangular opening in the wall about two feet by three feet. It was underneath the escalator hidden from view to the rest of the mall, so I peeked inside. It was a filthy little space where people had been working on the wiring underneath the escalators. It was really loud and dangerous with the escalator steps upside down above my head, and the crud that fell from them mostly collected in a small cleaning brush at the bottom but it was shelter from the cold.

I crawled inside and saw that there was a little corner that bent around the wall, and inside it was a little space about four feet by six feet that was directly under the escalator. The automatic steps chugged and spun right above my head, and there was an inch of dust from cut drywall and scum that had fallen off the escalator steps. There was also a canvas covering for something that was blanketed in dust and filth. I was beyond out of options at this point and figured I could at least stay out of the cold for the night.

I shook out the canvas as well as I could, but it was still a filthy mess, corroded and stif fas a board. I had nothing I could use for a pillow so I just curled up in a ball on the floor and listened to the chunky rhythm of the escalator until it turned off.

I couldn't sleep. The withdrawal from dope was making me shiver and it felt like there was fiberglass imbedded in my canvas covering, so I scratched all over. The only thing I could say was that I wasn't cold. I heard the security guards making their sweep through the building right over my head and shaking dust loose with each step. I knew as long as I was quiet I would escape detection, and I wondered if I snored if I fell asleep. I knew I didn't snore LOUD, but even the slightest noise would alert security to my presence. I was extremely uncomfortable anyway, so sleeping wasn't much of an option.

I felt even more like an idiot when the security guards were passing right over my head and my phone rang BRRRING! BRRRING!!!. I slapped it as quick as I could to shut it off and I knew they heard me. Their footsteps stopped right above me and I could faintly hear them talking to each other.

"Did you hear that?"

"Yeah, where did it come from?"

They were silent for a minute or so, and then I guess they decided they couldn't figure out where it was coming from and left the area.

About seven o'clock the next morning I waited until the coast was clear and then crawled out of my hole in the wall. Luckily there was a public bathroom on the upper level just one flight above me, so I bolted up the stairs to clean up. I couldn't believe what I saw in the mirror. I was covered head to toe in gypsum dust from the drywall that was laying in pieces around where I slept. My nice black suit pants and collared shirt looked like someone had rolled them in flour to go in the oven and I wasn't a pretty sight either. My eyes were red and swollen from the lack of sleep and particles in the air.

I started the birdbath ritual, washing from head to toe as quickly as possible before security came in and caught me. I didn't want to burn this spot out, I might need it again. I made it downtown and to work in as little time as possible, scoring the minute I got off the train and zipping right back to Hollywood the minute I had it. Getting to work early meant I could shoot up in the bathroom, clean up whatever I had left to clean, and maybe eat a little something before the meeting.

I saw my now ex friend who was supposed to let me stay, but I really didn't want to talk to him. I played it off like I had a million other friends. I didn't want it getting around work I was homeless, so I told him everything worked out okay and I had a place.

I spent whatever free time I had calling friends and seeing if I could get hooked up with a couch. No luck. I had used up those favors with people long ago. It was another week before I got paid, so I had a choice between getting a hotel room or getting dope. If I got a room, I would have a place to sleep but no dope. If I had dope, I wouldn't be sick but I'd be out on the street.

Dope won. I knew even if I had to crawl under the escalator again at least this time I could get high and not feel so cruddy. After work I stopped by my storage space and grabbed some fresh clothes along with some things to clean up with and a pillow.

I cleaned out my space under the escalator as quickly and as quietly as I could, put the blanket on the floor, set my pillow at the head, lit a small candle, and started to fix. With the candle lit I could see the room a little better and still didn't feel I was exposing myself. The candle light was too dim to be seen and I was behind a corner after you climbed in the wall. I shot my dope with a little satisfaction, feeling safe and warm.

I climbed in early so I could escape detection but that meant I was stuck there for the night. There was a small step down at my feet where the escalator disappeared into the ground. I crawled to the edge, took careful aim, and peed right into the abyss. The revolving stairs were missing my head by about two inches and I took care not to stand or crouch up- It would've given me a nasty bash, or what if my hair got caught in it?

I kept thinking how embarrassing it would be when they found my corpse ground to a red paste by the constantly revolving escalator or maybe my melon would get caught in the machinery and carry me up into the belly of the darkness that resides under all escalators, hanging my body like a dancing scarecrow, a rhythmic 'thump thump' heard as the steps go over what used to be my spinal column. I jiggle in time to the industrial beat of the escalator as the steps wear down my head like sandpaper, leaving only a rugby shirt collar and its contents on down.

You think about suicide a lot when you're a dope addict.

You think of creative and fast ways to end the pain.

You seriously consider attempting them.

The morphine flowing through my body gave me a wonderful rush and I felt the stress of the day lift off of me. Aside from a hard floor and dusty air I was safe and warm for the night, that was all I cared about. I knew this wouldn't last as a place to stay and kept racking my brain for a way out of this mess, but they all pointed to the same thing- I had to quit dope.

As hard as I tried, I just couldn't. That's how strong the addiction is. I would rather lay on a filthy floor underneath an escalator in a shopping mall than get straight and have an actual place to live. I consider myself a strong person. I worked my way through college, had my own business for a time, and traveled all over the world. I wasn't someone easily swayed by others' influence. Yet here I was, peeing on the ground near where I slept, in a hole in the wall under some stairs.

This was what I called home.

It would get far worse before it got better.

Every day I brought something with me- an extra blanket, another pillow, a bottle to pee in, a gallon to drink out of. I even had dishes that were starting to pile up. With about a half dozen candles burning, the place was starting to look like a real squat. I even told a couple junkie friends of mine about it and one of them even asked if he could move in with me. He was living on the street and usually slept under park benches or in alleys.

Alleys were especially disgusting because that's where homeless people went to the bathroom during the day, and the alleys near Skid Row were always decorated with plenty of shit and toilet paper. In the summer heat the stench is unbearable and layers of waste pile up until the hazmat crews come.

CHAPTER THIRTEEN

Toilets are readily available on Skid Row, though the only clean ones are safely behind lock and key in offices not meant for the homeless. There are several in the missions that have eight stainless steel urinals and no doors on the toilets. Too many junkies used to go in there to shoot up and too many nod off with the door locked. There is always the occasional overdose, and it isn't uncommon to see someone on the floor of the bathroom having his pockets rifled through by the other addicts nearby. To attempt to keep the area clean, the city installed portable bathrooms, the kind of large and easily cleaned toilets that they use at concerts and construction sites and installed several right on the sidewalks of Skid Row.

The portable single toilets in the parks stayed standing, but the ones on the sidewalks soon became coveted property for junkies, crack smokers, and heroin addicts who needed a place to prepare their works. Since there was a demand, someone was now constantly standing at the doors of these toilets demanding a dollar for every ten minutes the person wanted to use it. Hookers who charged only five dollars for a blowjob were especially keen on them since they were readily available to service customers with.

Junkies were less enthusiastic as the time it took to boil up your hit and find a vein could vary from five minutes to an hour or more. You need to have a comfortable well-lit environment to safely hit a vein and those just aren't available downtown. You need an apartment because unless you can fix lightning fast (or are ready to fend off the people trying to break down the toilet door after five minutes), you might not have enough time to get it right.

Soon people moved in the portable toilets and their hand washed clothes hung from strings they had taped up all over the insides of the units. Usually they had sealed the lid to the tank to try and curb the smell but it never helped in the slightest. They would scream, "HEY! THAT ONE'S MINE!" whenever someone opened the door to use the facilities and dove towards their treasured pile of clothes and whatever else it was that they had in there. They slept right inside of the bathrooms curled up on top of the seat, which usually had about fifteen layers of clothes, the door locked all night so that no one could use them, each one a little apartment that smelled horrible, but you can't beat the rent.

Soon of course those without toilets and the luxury of portable potty living became envious of those who lived inside of the toilets and since there was no lease or rent to be paid, fights broke out over ownership. No one could be there to watch their toilet twenty-four hours a day, so when they turned their backs that's when items were removed, then fighting broke out. Eventually most of the toilets were turned over and the contents were spilled out onto the streets, often with the resident trapped inside. The fecal, menstrual, urinal, and oral waste of hundreds of homeless people came swirling up the toilet as it was tipped to and fro, the panicked and screaming resident trapped inside and fearing the inevitable.

Soon it tipped over and the blue shit filled water and greenish urine came oozing out the sides, and the duct tape that held the door closed from the outside ensured a thorough bath for the resident who was unwilling to share the bounty of porta potty safety and luxury they had appropriated from the city. Sometimes it would land on its door and the person thrashing and screaming inside was trapped until someone took pity on them and kicked the toilet over on its side so that they could finally escape and beg people for water. They would rather destroy a useful item they could not be in possession of than to share it with others and chip in to keep it going and in good shape.

Finally, the hard-plastic toilets that were so desperately needed by the homeless to be able to go to the bathroom at night were torn to pieces, set on fire, and let burn to the ground. The blackened marks on the building stood for months. The city stepped up and installed quarter million dollar each, robotic, self-cleaning, timed private bathrooms with automated doors and complete hose down of the insides while it went into 'cleaning' mode between each user.

Junkies especially loved these because police couldn't get the door open from the outside without great effort. It could also fit about three junkies comfortably or five junkies uncomfortably. It was common to see small parties happening in the twenty minutes the robot bathroom allowed you before opening the door without warning. We all learned quickly if you are in there for the full twenty minutes police will often wait for the door to open so they can catch you trying to hide your dope.

CHAPTER FOURTEEN

The greatest accomplishments in this world are made by great leaders and great thinkers, people who are able to take the knowledge of the world up until that point and go a little bit further, stamping their name indelibly on a formula or measurement, plant, animal, or map coordinate, and remain a footnote in history forever. It takes an organization of people to create a cohesive, communal living environment that is able to function without the confusion of slaying each other, recruiting young men into the army by force, or riding horses down crowded alleyways with the secret police chopping off the heads of proletariat blue collar citizens.

For this, we have laws, we have locks on our doors, we have safe places to keep our things. We stake out our territory and claim it by whatever means necessary; it could be financial, it could be family, it could be blood, or murder, or coercion, fraud, or it just could be careful financial planning and common sense. Killing people for their land is what happens when you don't have people watching what you do. There are ALWAYS people willing to kill but are unfortunately bound by the constraints of society, so they stake their claim in other ways.

Now imagine all of your things are taken out of your house and thrown into the street. No matter what you did and how hard you tried, that eviction notice was served by the sheriff and your locks have been changed. You have spent what little money you had on a lawyer and exhausted what charity could be begged from friends and family. You sold what little valuables you had for pennies on the dollar to get a boot off of your car, or to pay for medicine, or to bail out your husband.

You try to keep an eye on things but slowly your goods disappear off of the street. You need to get out of here and you have no money and no one to help you. Pretty soon the local police come by and tell you to get the stuff off of the curb or the city will come by and take it. He also tells you that the neighbors are complaining that you are even still here.

How quickly they turn venomous when you are going down. How easily they turn their backs when you were always there for them, often putting yourself on the line to help someone out. You find out the hard way that the world is a cold place, and your mother is calling asking if you can pick up your children please she needs to go to work in a few hours and she cannot leave the children alone.

You ask if you can just watch the children for the time she works, and she says no, you were supposed to pick them up three days ago and you said you had everything under control. You make a half dozen calls, now older and older friends, begging for help and maybe even getting some, but it is not enough. You've let yourself slide too far down, you need way too much money to get everything back up to where it was just three days ago, when you had electricity, a bathroom, your own big fuzzy warm robe, your favorite records and cassettes you've been collecting since grade school, your expensive and hard won wardrobe, many things tailored by you, your children's first drawings, your Christmas and Hanukkah decorations, your wedding photos, the presents your mother gave you for graduation, all gone. Everything. Instantly.

You haven't hit bottom. Not by a long shot. You've just started a downward slide that has been building up for years. You've built up such a teetering hill of poor financial decisions, low paying jobs and desires that are beyond your resources that it all came crashing down on top of you all at once, and there is no digging out from it. Easily approved loans guaranteed you financial freedom but you had to put up your house as collateral. Those companies have no soul, they care nothing about you or your community. All of the bank owners live far, far away, usually in other countries, in a world of opulence and comfort you will never even get a chance to taste let alone join.

They create broadcast shows to allow you to feel like you're a part of it.

It's a fucking illusion.

You aren't a part of it, no one really is. The people on the shows are acting no matter how real it may seem.

They create characters larger than life, and the only reason people believe them is because they are conditioned to think, 'They're on television so they must be important. I'm sure that someone at the station screened their credentials".

Well, no.

When you buy into the news and media, you have no power to contribute to their conversation, and so you accept the decisions of people that you really don't know, to do things that you think are beneath you because your degree isn't in demand right now and accept a standard of living that could easily be paid for with a small sales tax, but they demand that you give up to half of your salary, money that you could use to keep a roof over your head, and they use that excess money to keep themselves in the lifestyles to which they have become accustomed.

You most likely can't talk to these people at all. Mega corporations broadcast just the same as governments and they are all using the same tactics now. They SEND you information. It is available on their website, or you can call customer service, THEY will tell you how to get help, and THEY will refer you to a website that will answer all of your questions.

Why was my house taken from me?

Sir, we sent you the link with the answers to all of your questions. It is unfortunate that you could not meet the payments that we were assured are affordable to you. We cashed our own check for you and trusted you at your word, it doesn't matter that your child was sick, it doesn't matter that you had to get your car fixed. It doesn't matter that your neighborhood is flooded with cheap and easily available drugs or that your kid is in jail for vandalism.

All that matters is that we loaned you the money, you didn't pay us back when you said you would, and now we have taken what you offered as collateral. If you did not understand the terms of the repossession, we would have been more than happy to meet with you to explain them thoroughly. As we were not aware that these conditions were not absolutely clear to you, we cannot make any changes to meet your unfortunate circumstances, which we were not aware of at any time.

As it is also after the fact that we have legally taken possession of the property in question, I must inform you that any attempt to regain control of the property or even to be on the property without our express permission is a violation of local laws and if necessary, we will prosecute.

If you have any possessions that you would like to reclaim, please fill out this form and you will be notified of when and where to retrieve them. As we have no idea what items may be in the property, we cannot accept this list as a factual claim of things that you wish to have us return to you, but as a request for assistance in returning goods that were abandoned, and therefore have no legal duties to recognize nor admit that any of the items on the list in fact exist, but if you tell us where the good shit is hidden, maybe we'll throw you a motherfukkin' bone.

Probably not though.

Sincerely,

Your foreign owned bank.

CHAPTER FIFTEEN

The homeless of Skid Row are in the country's lowest percentage literacy wise. Libraries and learning centers nearby offer plenty of adult literacy programs for free, but night after night the classrooms remain empty and the streets full as everyone turns up their music to overpower the other guy's radio. Blunts wrapped in a variety of cigar tobacco leaves are twisted and spit on to form beautiful little joints the color of paper shopping bags and smoked all day long and in such a variety of strains that the park on the corner smells like a marijuana dispensary.

There are an ample amount of services here for anyone who wants to utilize them and every opportunity for advancement is offered. The fact that I'm white has not been beneficial to me in any way and were I of a different color, there would have been MORE financial resources available to me. The mindset of the average Skid Row citizen is that money should come to them without effort, or at the most it should cost a few hours in a public service building.

While handouts and welfare have certainly been important in emergency situations, it has created a population of citizens completely unable to care for themselves.

I have always tried to volunteer when I have the extra resources. There are two dozen places down here that need volunteers daily and mostly they are staffed with the Skid Row residents. I talked to some women who taught inner city children. The problem is the same at the level I am familiar with as it is with the grade school level. There is very little incentive for them to learn, and even less encouragement. If a kid is raised in the right environment and provided mental stimulation, they will form a mind that is able to function at a very high level. If they are raised surrounded by fear, hatred, and mistrust, they will reflect that as well.

CHAPTER SIXTEEN

My downtown friends LOVED my new spot under the escalators in the Kodak Oscar Museum. Two of them came to stay with me. Can you imagine people were actually jealous of my situation? They thought it was a great spot and I had never looked at it from the perspective of an ACTUAL homeless person before. It wasn't much bigger that a walk-in closet, but you could stand up at one end and the other was where the escalator disappeared into the ground. All I had to do was walk around the mall until no one was looking then I just disappeared under the stairs and I was hidden for the night.

The only time I almost got caught was one night I couldn't score- there was no dope to be found ANYWHERE and I knew if I didn't get back to my spot in time the mall would close and I would be locked out. It sucked, but I knew I was just going to have to come back in the morning. I got back to my spot but the dope sickness was making me shiver and convulse. I was moaning, and I try to keep it to myself, but I guess I was moaning a little too loud.

I heard footsteps above me and I froze.

Somebody heard me, and they couldn't figure out where the noise was coming from.

I heard their thick heavy boots plod down the stairs to my landing, and they came around the corner back to the little hole in the wall which was my entrance. I could hear them breathing, and I was frozen.

I wasn't afraid of the security guards but the mall was locked for the night and if they found me and called the cops I would go to jail. I peeked around the corner to see if I could see anything and there he was, sticking his fat face in the little hole in the wall. I ducked back behind the corner where he couldn't see me and he turned on his mag lite to get a better look. I knew he couldn't see me around the corner, but if he saw those blankets and water jugs, I'd be busted for sure. He directed his beam left, then right, and slowly back again. Satisfied there wasn't some junkie living underneath the stairs of their multimillion dollar palace, he wandered off. Breathing a sigh of relief, I took a big hit of dope to celebrate not getting caught.

Funny thing about Heroin is that it's right for every occasion. Can't sleep? Take a hit. Can't get out of bed? Take a hit. Heroin is the only substance in the world where you can feel like shit because you did too much and take a little more and then feel better. Did too much coke or speed? Take a hit of heroin. Good day? Heroin. Bad day? Heroin. Tues day? Heroin

I had a paycheck to pick up and another one coming after that, so I was okay for a few weeks, if you consider living under an escalator in a shopping mall okay. I had enough money for dope and that was all that mattered. The job was teetering on the brink of quitting or being fired, so I split. Now I had free time to fuck around downtown all day if I wanted to.

First thing in the A.M. I'd go and score and usually meet up with one or two people I knew. A lot of them were already on the street and knew some good places to go and fix. I followed a few of them to a place they said was safe and it wasn't far away. You should be very, very cautious if someone ever asks you to do this. I trusted these guys, but I've also seen people get jumped pretty severely for their money or stash once they get out of sight of the main road.

Things like this usually turn out to be bad moves. Someone takes you to a parking lot bathroom or a parking stall where they think no one can see and you get busted. I was anxious to get high and I didn't want to wait until I got back to my spot, but I didn't want to fix on the train, either. I followed my friend up 5th Street on Broadway where we bought the dope, then walked past Pershing square and into the business district. They said they knew a good spot to shoot up where the police wouldn't see us.

I was sure this was a bad idea, so I was apprehensive the whole way. We kept going and walked up past the library to the other side of the Bonaventure Hotel on 4th and Figueroa. Right when I was about to ditch these guys and take my shit home, they yelled, "Here we are!!". We were on the other side of the freeway, at 4th and Beaudry near a chain link fence. The fence divided the freeway on ramp on the OTHER side of 4th street and on this side of 4th street it was a giant forested hillside with a few big trees and lots and lots of vegetation, neck high shrubs and vines covering the fence , all of which made it perfect for hiding and shooting up.

I liked it because it was away from all of the concrete and steel, away from the piss and shit filled alleyways a lot of the other junkies liked to shoot up in. I never understood that, but I can't imagine most people would understand my living situation either. There were hundreds of giant shrubs and dozens of small trees that made it easy for us to build little coves in where we would be hidden from view.

We picked out a spot that was perfect for the three of us to hit up in and we spread newspaper around us to keep from getting dirty. It was at the top of a slope that led down to the freeway beneath us and two hundred yards away were the buildings of the business district. It was the kind of view that people would pay thousands monthly for in high rent condos or lofts, but here it was, ours for free.

I shot up my supply and dozed off.

It was dark when I woke up. The dope made me pass out for the whole day.

"Oh, SHIT! WHAT TIME IS IT?!?!"

"About ten thirty. Why, you gotta be somewhere?"

"YEAH, I DO! HOW COME YOU GUYS DIDN'T WAKE ME UP?!?! "

"You didn't tell us to. Where do you gotta be?

"Ohhh, SHIT! If I'm not at my spot in half an hour, they lock it up! I'm not gonna make it! "

"So what? Listen, just crash right here. You can borrow my jacket because I got my blanket with me, and in the morning, we'll all go score together."

I had never considered sleeping outdoors but I had never been homeless before, either. Kindly accepting their generous offer, I flattened out some brush and grass and soon had a comfy little bed of green. The constant drone of the freeway made it easy to sleep plus the dope we had was pretty good. I felt safe there, too. There were trees with over hanging limbs that made it impossible to see us unless you were right next to us and the highway patrol rarely, if ever, got out of their cars to poke around by the freeway off ramp.

The next morning we went to score as usual but I went back to that spot by the freeway. I had some cash and threw my friend down a hit for showing me this place to sleep if I ever needed it. It turns out I would use it a great deal in the future, but back then I was ever hopeful that I would somehow get myself out of this situation. I had never applied for welfare or food stamps either, and he told me when I was totally out of money he would navigate me through the system. He said we could get food stamps the day we applied, and he knew how to turn those food stamps into cold hard cash. That one was a last resort.

In the meantime I was splitting my hours between downtown where I was scoring and Hollywood where my safe spot to sleep was. I also made a little extra money playing guitar out on Hollywood and Highland. It was right in front of the Mann's Chinese Theatre, so there were a thousand tourists who walked by.

The spot I played in was right next to the red line metro station so as soon as I got eight bucks I'd get a day pass for three dollars and zoom downtown to the Pershing Square stop which was where the dope was sold. I was making around ten bucks an hour, more than I made at the music store, and I could break whenever I wanted to so I could score.

The guitars I've had throughout my life have been amazing resources, and I never fail to keep one close by. Even in the worst of my homeless days, upon first having a small bit of extra cash the first thing I would buy was an acoustic guitar. The vibrations of the strings against my chest are very calming and I would sit for hours just focusing on one note and let it resonate through my body.

There was never a shortage of people who wanted to be close to a musician who could play well. Play in a busy section of town on a lazy afternoon, and you can make quite a bit of money too. I try not to get too attached to them as they are too easily stolen on the streets, but I could not easily count the amount of nights I spent with the neck of the guitar firmly wedged between my legs and one eye open for the ever present thieves.

This system was working out for a little while, then tragedy struck. I had my guitar with me everywhere I went, and I went up to my spot behind the Bonaventure freeway entrance ramp to fix. I was tired of carrying it around, so I stashed it behind the bushes thinking there was no way anyone could find it. I was only going to be gone a little while.

Sure enough, when I returned, it was gone. I was in tears. This wasn't some piece of crap pawn shop guitar, this was a Guild solid spruce top beauty that played like a dream and sounded just as good. I had a lot of guitar players tell me never to sell it. Everyone said it was one of the best sounding guitars they had ever played.

I bought it after a winning night at the riverboat casinos in the Chicago suburbs, so it had sentimental value as well. I never wrote down the serial number, but it has two very distinctive gouges on either side of the sound hole where I ripped the strings of fwith a monkey wrench in a drunken rage one night.

If anybody ever comes across a guitar like this, I would gladly pay a thousand dollars to get it back, no questions asked. That was the last acoustic guitar that I invested in. Every one since has been a cheap purchase. Today I play an Ibanez single cutaway hollow body that cost me $65. It sounds amazing.

CHAPTER SEVENTEEN

I had no way to make money and the cash I had from work was just about out. I needed a new hustle. I tried asking for spare change, but I was never good at it. There are guys I know who make two hundred dollars a day hitting people up for cash, but I never made more than a few bucks in an afternoon doing it so I knew that wasn't right for me.

If I raised a few bucks in Hollywood I would then spend the next hour and a half to two hours on the train downtown and back. That took up too much of my time that I could have been using to hustle. I had spoken to some friends who said there were beds available at the missions in Skid Row where they slept. I was also convinced there was more money to be made downtown.

Since all of the dope dealers were down there anyway, I packed up what few things I had, took the train downtown, showed them my I.D. at the Union Mission at 6th and San Pedro in the middle of Skid Row and got myself a thirty-day bed pass. I had officially hit almost bottom. I was now a homeless drug addict resident of Skid Row. The only things beneath this were jail and death, and they were always hovering close by.

CHAPTER EIGHTEEN

The Union Rescue Mission is populated with guys who are right out of prison, jail, rehab, mental hospitals or crisis centers;. Naturally the first crime they turn to is stealing from one another, and I kept what few possessions I had close by. There were about one hundred and twenty bunk beds in the room I was in, I think it was an old basketball court.

I looked at the faces of the old men and asked myself, "Is this how I'm going to wind up? Am I going to be here for the rest of my life? Am I going to be in and out of jail, unable to quit using dope and constantly stealing from friends and family? Will I be constantly moved from institution to institution, forever on a hamster wheel of fear and lack of control of my life until I finally suffer my remaining years in a place like this, on a filthy mattress with some poetic younger guy looking at me and hoping with every ounce of his being that he doesn't wind up like me?

CHAPTER NINETEEN

Skid Row was about a six-block square are of downtown Los Angeles that started from about 3rd street to seventh street north to south, Los Angeles boulevard to Central Avenue east to west. Within that area there were three missions, the Los Angeles mission, the Union Mission, and the Midnight Mission, all of which had beds. There were a few other scattered places that set up beds for the night in outdoor parking lots and indoor cafeterias, and I think these places were funded by the state, but they changed back into parking lots and cafeterias around six a.m.

Within this territory were rows of tent cities, some of which were taken down first thing in the morning, and some of which were allowed to stay up all day. The spots where you could keep your tent up all day were well protected and coveted by the others who had to take their tents down, because if you could keep your tent up it meant you could collect a little property, or sell drugs in the tent during the day, or charge people to use your tent to do drugs, and there were many other benefits.

The police used to make certain sections roll up their tents in the A.M., but around 2013 the ACLU got involved and demanded that the city allow homeless citizens to be able to keep up their tents all day. Insisting that carrying them around in order to keep them from being stolen was deemed unreasonable and cruel, and the homeless now are able to keep their tents up twenty four hours a day.

The tent cities have turned into mini neighborhoods and the tents sport such luxuries as barbeque grills, microwaves, and little stores where the homeless sell old pairs of sneakers and small items that were shoplifted. They also block the sidewalks with a ton of leftover garbage that attracts rats. There is usually a person who is assigned to be block monitor and keep all of the fire hazards to a minimum. They aren't always doing their job, and the clutter gathers up into refuse piles that grow in size, stench, and contamination right in the street. The tents also provide the perfect shelter for criminals, and the police are often seen shining flashlights into the flaps and entrances of the tents while looking for a suspect.

The Homeless mental health facility was on 5th and Maple and you could go in there and get prescription drugs like Seroquel or Xanex which then sold on the street for a buck or two each. Down on 4th and Towne was the needle exchange where you could either get fresh ones for yourself or sell sealed ones on the street for a dollar apiece. Across the street from that was a recycling station, probably the worst one in the world. You could collect cans all day and go there and get a dollar twenty-five a pound and it was around twenty-two cans to a pound.

That area of the block was also a pickup station for day workers in the morning. If you wanted a job for the day you could go there about four o'clock in the morning when some vans would pull up that were looking for workers. Usually it was companies that handed out coupon fliers or newsprint advertisements for places like Home Depot or Sears, and you would walk around neighborhoods rubber banding them to people's gates or throwing them in their driveways. It was hard work, and you began at 4 a.m. when the vans pulled up. If you were lucky enough to be selected for the day, you'd be back by twelve thirty with maybe thirty dollars in cash. That was enough to stay well.

The next day you'd get up and start all over again.

CHAPTER TWENTY

The other thing that made this area so attractive to the homeless is the FOOD. If you were homeless in Los Angeles you didn't go hungry unless you wanted to. Between the three missions, a few churches scattered around the place, and donor trucks that pulled up daily with a ton of food, there was plenty to eat, and it really wasn't that bad, either.

It started at five-thirty a.m. with breakfast at the Los Angeles mission. You had to be there on time or they shut the gate in the front. Then you had to sit through a half hour mass with most everyone was still asleep in their chairs. At the end of the sermon, you were served some oatmeal and bacon with toast and juice. It wasn't a feast, but it was enough to fill your stomach.

At six o'clock people got in line for the Midnight Mission breakfast that started at seven. There was a small car that pulled up another block away that showed up at six thirty with the leftover Krispy Kreme doughnuts from yesterday, two hundred doughnuts per box, all in messy rows. They fed about five to eight hundred people every morning, so it was a long line, but well worth it.

French toast with sausages were not uncommon, scrambled eggs with bacon or fresh fruit you got at least once a week, and every morning there were thousands of day old Krispy Kreme doughnuts. Sugar glazed or chocolate with cream filling, they were a favorite of everyone's and if you stood by you could collect as many uneaten ones as you could carry. At nine o'clock they served another breakfast at the Union Mission. It was like this for lunch and dinner, too. You only went hungry in Los Angeles if you wanted to.

CHAPTER TWENTY-ONE

The next morning they wake you up at around five thirty, give you a half an hour to get your shit together and toss you in the street. I never understood why they made us leave so early. It was cold outside so the only thing to do was to sit in the chapel area downstairs. If you had a bed pass they didn't make you leave the premises, just the sleeping area.

The chapel was anything but comfortable. You sit in an auditorium with banners on the walls of incomprehensible bible quotes; "Let him who follows thee repent and the way of the flock is guidance for all men, that they should live and be well in the manner of the Lord". They didn't want people sleeping in the chapel so they played gospel music full blast.

The other option was to hit the street. It was still dark out and chilly enough to make me usually want to stay where it was warm in winter months. Some of the guys in there were dope dealers so they got to work early. There was a huge amount of traffic for this time of morning. Everyone wanted to get their fix before work, so the crack and heroin trades were well under way.

I was totally out of cash. All I had was my backpack with a few clothes. I had already sold or pawned anything in my storage space that was worth any money, and even though I had a lot of nice recording equipment stashed away I couldn't get myself to hock it. I wanted to keep it for whenever I got out of this mess. Besides it was way too heavy to carry. There were a few options to make money down on Skid Row and most of them were illegal. I wasn't ready to go to jail just yet, so I pulled a garbage bag out of a can and started picking up aluminum and plastic. This would be my job for the next two months.

Recycling gives you a small sense of dignity. It was honest work, it was helpful to the environment, and it was something that the more you hustled, the more you made. I was on the west side of downtown by ten o'clock in the morning. Water bottles littered the streets by the thousands, and aluminum cans were plentiful as well. I soon had a section of town called Santee Alley as my territory, and it was a gold mine for recycling.

Santee Alley was an outdoor shopping plaza between Olympic Boulevard and Pico where they had hundreds of little shops that sold everything from fake Rolex watches and Gucci purses to little robot toys and designer perfumes. It reminded me a lot of the Turkish bazaars that held thousands of little shops, each under a small awning made of a decorative and colorful sheet. Santee Alley was like that minus the cultural overload.

In the mid -afternoon hours the sun blazed down on the shoppers and they drank thousands of gallons of soda and water. This was where I came in. I circled the place with my trash bag, digging through and emptying the trash containers of their plastic bottles and aluminum cans. When I had enough for the recycling center I walked about ten blocks to cash them in. There were two recycling centers near downtown, and they were both run so poorly it was a wonder they stayed in business at all.

Usually in the early afternoon there was someone there and I could get six bucks for my morning hit. In the afternoon, as many times as not they said, "The guy with the cash isn't here. I don't know where he is. You can wait here or come back later." I had a choice of either waiting around for the guy to show up or running ten blocks to the other recycling center where the same thing could happen.

Sundays were the worst. One of the places was closed and the other didn't open until six p.m. People started lining up at around noon, so if you got there at six you had at LEAST a three hour wait until they got to you. One guy even started coming early with cash of his own and buying people's recyclable material for less than half of what it was worth and then cashing it in on his own later. He easily cleared a couple of hundred a day. That was fucked up, taking advantage of junkies like that, but if they didn't want to wait they could sell and get 50% of the cash. I'm sure this was done with the full cooperation of the re cycling center, who probably got a cut to stay closed for a little bit longer.

The important thing was to get to the recycling center and get your cans and bottles cashed in before curfew. They shut down Santee Alley at six o'clock, which meant I had two hours to get to the recycling center, wait in line, cash out my cans and bottles, and get to a dealer before I had to be at the Mission at eight o'clock. Usually there were dealers who circled close to the recycling centers knowing that half of the people cashing out would want either crack or heroin, so four out of five days you could score easily.

The fifth day, there was always a problem. You couldn't take your bag of cans to the mission with you so you HAD to get rid of them. It was also impossible to stay outdoors with them until morning, because if you missed a night at the mission, you lost your bed. It didn't matter if you had a medical emergency, a relative die, or were in jail, if you didn't show up, you lost your bed. Twenty five out of thirty days of the month the mission had a sign, NO BEDS AVAILABLE, so you never wanted to risk losing your spot.

Sometimes the lines were too long, and you had to sell to one of the brokers in line who gave you half price. The guys who ran the place were NOTORIOUSLY slow, counting each and every nickel, dime, and quarter they gave out on their fingers. The recycling center on Alameda street was much quicker, but it was another ten blocks walk to get there so you had to RUN with a twenty-pound bag under each arm. It was also in the middle of nowhere so you had to run the ten blocks back to get to a dealer. If they were both closed, you had to find a place to stash your day's work and pray it would still be there in the morning.

There were a few peaceful moments on Skid Row, and one or two places to relax that made you forget you were living here. In the early afternoon there is a park that opens up on 5th and San Julian, a little corner of grass and a few tables that people play cards or dominoes on. They installed a half dozen portable toilets for people to use, so whenever I came up with a few dollars and could take the rest of the day off, I would go in the toilet, cook up my stash, shoot up, and lay down in the grass or sit and talk to people I knew.

They kept the park in good shape, cleaning it every day when they closed and again when they opened so it was the one outdoor spot in all of Skid Row that wasn't full of trash or smelled like urine or feces. There were a few trees scattered around so you could get a little shade and radios were banned so you got a little peace and quiet. I often fell right asleep on the grass and dreamed of better days.

CHAPTER TWENTY-TWO

Soon I was into a little routine that kept me busily flowing through Skid Row. Wake up at five. Breakfast at seven, score dope or enjoy one I had from last night, get to work by nine or ten, collect cans and bottles all day, score more dope, in bed and lights out by eight thirty. Keeping busy was a really crucial part of it. If I sat for too long and looked around at the filth I was living in and the way I was beginning to look, act, and smell, I would've really freaked out.

Pulling yourself out of a homeless situation is a long and difficult process. Jobs are harder to come by because not having a mailing address or someplace you can shower whenever you need to are major obstacles. I had the luxury of a cell phone, but at the time ninety nine percent of the people on Skid Row only had access to pay phones, so there is nowhere for an employer to call you back.

A large percentage of the people are without any kind of valid state I.D. making it difficult to apply for social services, jobs, or even beds in the missions which require state I.D. There are some programs available, but most of them are inpatient drug rehabilitation centers and are poorly planned. The goal of these services is supposed to get people back on their feet, but most of what I saw were attempts at religious conversion, state funded program managers milking the state for as much money as they could get out of each person they signed up for services, and medical programs that gave out prescription medication for mental illnesses that were improperly diagnosed, much less evaluated to the point of giving them the proper medication before sending them back out on the street completely wasted on Seroquel or some other anti-anxiety medication.

If the state really wanted to help the homeless, it should have a program run more like a corporation, where the homeless could come in and work or get job training and some kind of easy access banking specifically for the homeless so they could begin to build, a dollar at a time. Money in your pockets is easily spent or lost on the streets but having enough for a bank account or to start any kind of savings is nearly impossible, especially for those with any kind of drug addiction.

What keeps many people at the bottom is the fact that drugs are illegal. Most of the addicts I met on Skid Row are harmless, semi intelligent people who are not thieves, nor are they con artists, gangsters, or would ever do anything to hurt anyone else, yet they are criminals because they are addicted to drugs or were caught with a minimal amount. Most of them had criminal records for possession or petty theft due to addiction.

The police are quick to arrest people for victimless crimes such as possession, and those that are arrested often do thirty or more days for negligible amounts of narcotics. This is making criminals out of people who have a disease, and every day we are finding better and better ways of treating this disease. Jail is not the answer. It only adds to the problem of homelessness by keeping people from good jobs, keeping their money going through the courts to the state or to legal fees, taking up so much time and money, making it difficult to actually get back on track. No, the state works backwards in getting people of fthe street. In fact, it is probably just as responsible for keeping people homeless as drugs or unemployment.

The welfare system in Los Angeles County is called General Relief or GR. It is available for those who qualify, and amounts to about $220 a month in cash, and another $170 in food stamps. I saw almost everyone I knew who had this program spend all of their money on drugs. There were ways of cashing in your food stamps and you got back fifty percent of what you gave the cashing service in stamps. If you brought in $100 in food stamps, you got back $50 cash.

The GR office also supplied you with a two-week hotel voucher for one of the Single room occupancy hotels that are scattered across Skid Row. I had been staying in the mission for nearly a month at that point, so I was about to be kicked out on the street anyway. A friend told me where to go to apply, so I grabbed my I.D., hit myself up with a few bags to last the day (I knew it was going to be about a six hour process) and head for the welfare office on sixth and Park View, across the street from MacArthur Park.

The office was packed with applicants. Everyone seemed to have at least one child clinging to them. It resembled some kind of chaotic day care center. My name was called after about an hour of waiting, and I was really dope sick. I had been holding this off as a last resort because it felt (& for lack of a better word,) cheap. I had never asked for any kind of financial help in my life, but the constant enthusiasm of people I knew getting their $390 at the beginning of each month talked me into it.

It was a process with a hundred questions, all of them geared towards fine tuning the ergonomics of the homeless situation in Los Angeles. After about four hours of waiting, questioning, fingerprinting, and paperwork, I was granted an ATM card that would hold my future assistance money, and the food stamp money was in there instantly. I had a friend waiting outside in McArthur park for my completion, and the minute I was finished we were off and running to get the food stamps cashed in.

We went to the little food store on Fifth and San Julian, a convenience store that served a constantly changing buffet of baked chicken, macaroni and cheese, spaghetti and pasta, and other dishes that were actually not bad. They cooked in bulk, and it was a favorite eating spot for the homeless when you had a few extra bucks and didn't want to wait for the mission food. They also cashed in food stamps, so a few minutes after our arrival I had $50 in cash.

It was closer to the dealers down here than to run up to Broadway, so we walked a few blocks south to Gladys street. I hated going down there. The street was nothing but factories and fish canneries, and the stench from the rotting fish was unbearable. Garbage covered the street- not just residual trash, but people here turn over every can on the street looking for anything of value, so trash is piled high.

People were shooting up and smoking crack right in the middle of the street, in the doorways of their tents and in burned out cars parked on the side of the road. As soon as a new person walks on the street, people mob you from all sides trying to get a piece of whatever you are there for.

The usual deal is that if someone sets you up with a piece of crack or a balloon of heroin, they got either a few bucks or a little bit of the dope. The more they got for you, the bigger their commission. The dealers liked it this way so anyone they didn't know dealt with the middlemen instead of them and took all the risk of getting arrested if it was an undercover.

You could never trust ANYONE, because as often as not they will sell you a piece of wax wrapped up in foil. My friend knew who to look for, and we were able to get six nice sized and good quality heroin balloons from the main dealer on the street. You have to be careful who you talk to as well, because even if you say hello and "who's got dope?" to someone, they will STILL demand a cut, or a dollar, and they can get pretty aggressive about it. I learned early not to talk to anyone, just walk down the street until you see who you're looking for. If you strike out, slowly turn around and walk back.

I went to the social services building, and after a few hours of paperwork I had a hotel voucher. This meant I could stay at one of the hotels on Skid Row for two weeks free of charge. There were a few options, one was the Ross Hotel, located on sixth and San Julian. This was a pretty big place, probably about one hundred rooms, a cafeteria, and a medical center on the first floor. It was also a permanent residence for people on Social Security, section 8 and other government programs. The problem with this was that since people were living there permanently, the blacks there had developed their own hierarchy system, and a sort of unofficial rank was given to people based on seniority.

I had heard horror stories of people getting robbed, shaken down, even raped. The people who have lived there a long time have had opportunities to get spare keys to rooms so that when someone new moves in, they have access to their room and when they step out, they go through their stuf flooking for anything valuable. You had to go through metal detectors coming in to the building, and drugs were dealt openly outside the entrance. I had no desire to stay there.

The other option was the Panama, a smaller hotel just outside the park on fifth and San Julian. They only had about seventy rooms, and it was a little bit calmer. The bedrooms were like dorms, and there was a common shower/ bath area, but it was a little bit more home like atmosphere with less room to move, but this made it easier for security to keep an eye on what was going on. Since there was a room available at the Panama, I gratefully took the voucher and moved in.

CHAPTER TWENTY-THREE

It was luxury. Compared with the jail like atmosphere of the missions. Having your own room was a giant step up. I could now stretch out and relax a bit and not have to worry about getting caught shooting up. I spread my needles and works out on the small desk that was provided, and since I had a few more bucks from my food stamps, I re-upped my supply and lay in bed for two days watching t.v., eating, and snuggling myself to sleep in a thick warm blanket. They also served breakfast, lunch, and dinner in the common area, so all I had to do was roll out of bed, walk downstairs, and eat. This was a little more like it. I knew in two weeks I would be right back out on the street, but I decided not to worry about it now, relax, and enjoy my privacy.

One of the main difficulties I had to deal with on Skid Row was racism. I was raised in a very culturally diverse neighborhood, and my friends were Japanese, Jewish, Black, East Indian, and about everything else. I was raised to judge people by their actions and words, not by their color. Not everyone was raised this way, and I was getting the bad end of it.

It seems to black people who confronted me about it, whites have all the opportunities which they feel that they are denied, therefore anything the state gives away to the less fortunate is rightfully theirs. This isn't a theory I came up with, this is what I was told in many different ways by the blacks who lived on Skid Row. I was generally treated like an outsider. I was told point blank to my face I had no right to be there, because I was white I could go and get a job and food and shelter supplied by the government was meant for those that COULDN'T get a job because they were black.

Racism even permeated my living arrangement. It was so infuriating that it made me very bitter. It also helped me see what it is like to be prejudged, to have people hate you for your skin color. For right now, I wanted a better and faster way to come up with cash. I needed a better hustle. Recycling isn't a hustle, it's a last resort, but you gotta start somewhere.

The most coveted position to have on the street is to be the dope man, the street dealer. The gang that ran the heroin trade in the early 2000's on Broadway was the Fifth and Hill gang. The Fifth and Hill gang was started in the early 70's at the corner of 5th and Hill Streets where day laborers gathered at the time to find work. After a number of the laborers were assaulted the group banded together for protection. As time went on, they kept that ball rolling, now they were an actual force to be dealt with.

There was a huge supply chain that started in South America and worked its way up to supply the streets of The United States with heroin, marijuana, and cocaine. The fact that they were in control of the main heroin suppliers for downtown Los Angeles meant that they were moving more street dope than anyone else in the world. They protected their salesmen by giving them watchdogs, little kids who looked over the streets for undercover police and customers, as well as supplied them with whatever else they needed, girls, weapons, insurance.

The entire crew that led the street team were all solid guys. It was almost always a gang member who was the pack man, but the individual salesmen were usually Mexican street junkies or immigrants wanting to make quick cash or pay off a debt to a coyote and were therefore expendable. Gang members could be counted on for other things, addicts were only good for selling dope, stealing stuff, and buying dope.

There were the youngsters who idolized the older members and did whatever they said without question. To refuse was to get a beating, and I mean they got a BEATING. Black eyes, split lips, and other signs of discipline were fairly common amongst the younger kids, but there was a major difference between what was happening here in the gangs and what was commonly called discipline.

It broke my heart to see kids as young as ten and eleven out on the streets pushing dope, but all too often it isn't their choice. I see a lot less of it these days as the main dope areas are places with no stores and the only people who walk down those streets are addicts themselves. Usually the only time kids that young ever went on the street to sell was when everyone else was in jail and couldn't be there to make decisions.

Then there were the enforcers, the ones who dealt out punishment and discipline, the ones who collected the money. I always made sure to count out loud how much I was giving them right in front of their faces, usually in a garage on the hood of a car with at least one other person present. The enforcers aren't known for having a lot of patience, nor are they known for being fast or accurate at math, so you had better count carefully. If you're not shooting your mouth of fand bringing money in, they're easy to get along with.

The upper level guys you never see. They make the calls based on experience and current needs and tolerate no dissent in their ranks. All too often one of the guys in charge of the street gets busted, then they have to rearrange workers, figure out who can be trusted with that much cash, who the pack man will be, etc. No matter how bad things get, they won't go down to do mid-level jobs. They will promote someone from below to take up the slack and it goes by who is most dependable, cool headed, good with money, etc.

These guys have already done their time and won't take risks unless it is absolutely necessary, but they have the connections and respect to get a lot of things done that the younger people can't. I'm sure there are many more levels in the hierarchy but since we were at a street level, that's all that were visible to us. In all honesty, that's all I wanted to know.

CHAPTER TWENTY-FOUR

There were usually at least a half dozen or so workers selling balloons filled with heroin on the street, endlessly walking back and forth in front of clothing stores and pizza shops until their shift is over. These are without fail Latinos, mostly recent immigrants who didn't have much of a choice for jobs so they had to take high risk illegal work. They also employed one white guy to sell to white people who drove or took the train in from the suburbs, people who were hesitant to buy from Latinos that they didn't know.

There were always white people downtown to buy dope and many of them were addicts, but few wore the ragged clothes and falling apart shoes of the Skid Row junkie. They also usually came in twos and threes, so two white people with clean clothes, skateboards and backpacks in a drug area were a pretty obvious pair just asking to get busted. Once anyone looking clean cut stepped into our part of town, everyone on the block was looking to rip them off because they knew these kids had money and knew that they didn't have any friends down here to bail them out of danger.

Naturally, the more people got ripped off, the less came down, and pretty soon you're losing out on a couple of thousand dollars a day. To combat this money losing leak in the boat they kept one white guy on the street sales crew. The guy they had on their crew now was Joe, a short white guy with a dodgy mustache that made him look like he should work selling kebobs out of a stall, not dealing smack to scared white kids. He had the top slot for any white guy on the street, a gang to protect him, and looked like Nintendo's Italian video game star, Mario. We were all envious of him. Joe sold way more than his share of dope, and shot twice as much as he sold. I was always trying to hustle much needed dope money and it was a day to day existence, but Joe had plenty of cash on hand and was always nodding off from the three or four balloons he shot at one time.

The first thing I tried to make money was flyering. That's where you get up at three thirty in the morning, stand around the corner of 4th and Towne in Skid Row, and trucks would pull up and take you to some remote suburb, give you a shoulder bag filled with paper advertisements, and you walked a ten-square block area rubber banding flyers to people's houses. It was for things like Home Depot sales, coupon books, and pizzeria advertisements. You got paid about thirty dollars for working from five a.m. until one in the afternoon. By then it was too hot to continue. I had carried golf bags as a kid, sometimes thirty-six holes a day, two bags each round, and made some decent money, so I wasn't afraid of hard work. If this was all I could get, so be it.

When I showed up at four A.M. to look for work I felt like I had stepped into another dimension. It was my first time out on Skid Row in the middle of the night and it was an entirely different world than it was during the day. The people had turned from a huddled mass of tent living homeless people into something out of "The Wiz". Men dressed in garbage bag plastic and beer can sunglasses, cross dressing queens sat in the middle of the street with their boom boxes cranked full blast. Fires lit up the circles of people dancing and rapping and playing drums and fucking and smoking crack and crystal meth and going in and out of the tents, in and out, in and out, all night long. It was a party of the dancing dead worthy of a Tim Burton film.

Girls naked as the day they were born were dancing to music that seemed to come from every single corner of the ghetto, and each boom box played a different rap song at a different tempo, adding a bizarre electronic soundtrack to a true to life post apocalyptic nightmare. The people on either side of the street had portable rechargeable sound systems and they were all pumped up at full blast. The blue and red LED's on the outside of the amplifiers jumped up and down to the music, and several of them had mic inputs that sputtered and crackled as they tried in vain to get the microphones working. The lighters for crack pipes constantly flickering and glowing reminded me of firefly mating season in Michigan.

I began to see the reason they keep people as crowded as possible in these ghettos. The insanity of being in such close proximity is that you're always in someone else's business, and they're always in yours no matter how quiet you try to keep everything. They see every visitor, they see what time you get up and how you dress, they see who you bring home at night and who leaves in the morning. They hear your fights, they hear you fucking, they mean no harm, but at the same time you feel like you are always being watched, and you are.

This is a mental mind fuck that keeps people on edge. If they're on edge, they aren't relaxed and thinking properly. If they aren't thinking properly, they make dumb moves and wind up blowing their money on dope, or landing in jail, or passing around STD's like it was New Year's eve every night. This planned paranoia is meant to keep a large segment of the population down and the people who designed it don't even have to put in any work. It's designed so that once the people move in to this cramped, swollen, diseased and constantly in motion psychological experiment, all of the paranoia inducing actions are created by themselves, and the people who watch to see what happens don't even have to get involved.

The residents who live there ALL feel the pressure of another presence watching them or listening to them twenty four hours a day simply because the walls are so thin that you can hear every word being said in the next room. Pretty soon you listen to what they are saying, and feel like THEY are listening to you, when nothing could be further from the truth. Most of the fights I see and hear are about someone getting in someone else's business, and the rooms in the ghetto are designed that way.

The hotel I was in, The Panama, was always getting the two-week vacation strays and since there were people in there for long stays and people in there for short stays. The people who came with the two-week vouchers were always under suspicion since no one knew them, and they usually arrived fresh out of prison. I arrived alone and instantly felt like I had made a bad move. It was like an 80's movie where the record scratches across the surface and everyone stops what they're doing and stares at you.

It was going to be a rough two weeks.

CHAPTER TWENTY FIVE

The next morning I went out at four a.m. to see if I could find work on one of the flyering trucks. At about quarter after four, my friend's boss came rolling up. There was the usual rush for the door, but my buddy shoved everyone aside and threw me in the rear of the van. It already had four people in back he brought with him, and they were fast asleep. We drove on to the freeway and out of sight of the city, and the drone of the car put me to sleep for a few minutes.

When I woke up, we were far out in the suburbs. I had no idea what city we were in but after an hour of driving we rolled into a coffee and doughnut shop. We all got out, introduced ourselves, and the driver bought us all breakfast. I introduced myself, and my friend told him I had been doing this sort of thing for years and I was a seasoned pro. The driver took out a map, circled the area we were supposed to stay in and started to load up our bags with flyers.

We were supposed to walk throughout a subdivision up and down each street rubber banding flyers to each entrance gate, front door, or fence that surrounded each middle-class house. He loaded us up with as much as we could carry, gave us his cell number, and told us he'd be back to find us in about three hours.

We didn't have to look far to find fresh apricots, grapefruit, plums, and especially oranges. I wouldn't consider it stealing since there were over ripe and rotten ones on the ground in the yards we took from and they were obviously going to waste. We stocked up on fresh fruit and continued to eat while we talked and passed out flyers. It was so peaceful and energetic and beautiful in the suburbs that I thought I could do this for a while. It was good exercise, you got out of Skid Row for a bit, and there was fresh fruit for breakfast- really, really good fruit. Plus, I was finished by one o' clock in the afternoon so I had the rest of the day to do what I wanted and thirty dollars for two days' worth of dope.

Before I knew it we were being picked up by our driver, driven back to the downtown area, and I had thirty dollars. He said he only worked twice a week but if he saw me on those days, I could work for him. I grabbed my cash and flew to Broadway, picked up my dope for the day, went to my room, fixed, and went to the park on 5th and San Julian to lay down and talk to the regulars who sat there.

CHAPTER TWENTY SIX

The grass park on San Julian in Skid Row is a seemingly innocuous rest area, a place where the homeless can sit for a while and not worry about how bad their lives are. If you grew up in an area like I did, a suburb that had a lot of open area, trees and space, your parks were much different than if you grew up in the city, and light years away from the park on San Julian.

We had no fences around our parks, and they were immense. Usually they were large enough to contain a regulation football field, and not uncommonly they were the size of a polo field. That's I think about six city blocks. The grass was always watered and manicured, the baseball diamond raked and covered, and the worst the police ran into was a couple of kids smoking herb, and they usually sent them on their way with a warning.

The blasts we heard in my neighborhood weren't from guns but from kids with firecrackers. Any helicopters overhead usually held a public official, news crew, or cartographer, and they certainly did not shine their floodlights on you and tell you to freeze when you're walking along the sidewalk minding your own business. Children were allowed to go to the park on their own and were sent to bed with a scolding if they stayed out way past dark. Teenagers worried about their looks, not their lives.

Kids who grew up in the city had very different parks, schools, and neighborhoods. The parks in the cities were often just blacktop parking lots painted with a basketball court (or more commonly half of one), they were so small you couldn't play any games without running into other guys playing another game, and tension and conflicts ruined any chance of fair play. The homeless sat all day long in the corners of inner city parks, making it unavailable for parents to leave their children alone to play while they took care of other duties.

Garbage festered in corners where shrubs and flowers should be growing, and large tubular steel frames replaced cyclone fencing in the 90's, but neither of those surrounded the parks and gardens where I played football, baseball, and soccer in the Chicago suburbs. All of our equipment was state of the art, and all of the rules were watched over by referees and parents. There is rarely an adult supervised game going on in the city parks and the kids who were able to organize themselves into teams always wound up fighting with other children who were either at the park to cause trouble or were simply playing another game which collided with the other kids.

With no parents around to referee, conflicts broke out and with no one to stop them, they often escalate into violence.

There might be a water fountain, a few bleachers for others to sit on, the one in Hollywood even had a pool, but they weren't places you could find a quiet bench and study for an exam. They weren't places you could let your dog off of the leash and throw frisbees for him all day long.

The parks in inner cities are created in a way to make sure the kids who play in them feel familiarity with prison yards. The ghettos are designed to keep the impoverished down by creating the perfect storm of paranoia and psychological preparation for a life of slavery and imprisonment. I firmly believe this and can see it with my own eyes. I think that the reason they keep the poor in these conditions is to make sure that the jails stay full, and with that comes the inability to get ahead. Schooling is disrupted, money goes to the courts instead of to prom, and the cycle of poverty and crime perpetuates itself over and over again.

CHAPTER TWENTY SEVEN

The corner on San Julian is typical of an inner-city park. The park is incredibly small, about the footprint of a small apartment building, and would be impossible for children to find any room to play anything other than hopscotch on the hard concrete surface that covers most of the ground. There is little to no grass, and what is there is usually dead except for one month a year they lay new grass in and the sprouts are roped off. After a month the ropes are taken down and there is grass to lay on for a few short weeks. Luckily, there are very few if any children allowed to stay in Skid Row; it has the largest concentration of registered sex offenders in the world, and children do not belong here. Those that do come with parents are closely watched, something I'm silently grateful for.

I remember the first time I saw the giant bars around the perimeter of the park. I thought it looked like a prison yard. They want the poor to accept that they are prisoners, that they BELONG in prison. When they get to an actual prison, they see the concrete floors of the yard, hard iron benches, chain mail on the basketball nets, and without having to verbalize it, the man who was raised in an inner city with parks that are almost identical will instantly feel at home. The man who is raised in open spaces will feel confined and stressed.

The first man, who is raised in tightly confined buildings with very little privacy is automatically used to this setting, but doesn't realize that he's been conditioned to it without his knowledge. The second man will spend whatever money he has, beg, borrow, or steal, to get out of that place. This is another aspect of the conditioning. We see it on television every day. Shows that portray minorities as criminals brainwash and condition white people with money to believe that minorities ARE criminals, so when they land in a jail or prison, they instantly feel that they are surrounded by criminals. Yes, they are because they're in a jail, but it also applies to minorities that they meet in the world outside of jail.

This adds to the problem of racial inequality, and the fact that inner city youth buy into the myth that in order to be a hero or rap star you need to be a criminal feeds into that order perfectly. The fact that they brag and boast openly about crimes they commit and get away with, or how violent they are simply adds to an already fixed system.

The real crime is how they don't see that this too, is self perpetuating, and the fact that they buy into it makes it all too easy for police to arrest them, for society to turn away from them, and for minorities to see themselves as criminals. Since they are treated as criminals, they dress and act like criminals, they idolize and respect criminals, it's only a matter of time before they begin to commit crimes. Can they stay quiet about it? No, that's not part of the plan. The more crimes they commit, the more they have to let people know in order to get respect, and by using social media to let people know, they admit to more and more crimes on the internet. Little do they know that is admissible in court, and one after the other, put themselves in jail.

CHAPTER TWENTY EIGHT

There is way more than enough room within ninety minutes of any major city to build an enormous single dweller of single family home with a yard for those who are willing to put in the work to make it happen. Give them a reward system to build their houses. For anyone who wishes to apply, give them a job and goals within that job to add pieces to the house so that they can watch it grow online, and when enough time and/or money has been added by the person to balance the building of the house and pay for the material, they begin construction on a small plot of land the owner will keep as his yard.

There is a way to get this done. The technology is there, the people who are willing to educate the homeless on how to get themselves together financially are there, people like me who donate their time to show the homeless how to use the internet are there, but what is missing? Prefabricated and 3D printed houses are available for as little as $5000 and can be built in a single day. Most of the building is completely automated.

What's missing is approval from city council members. What's missing is someone with enough brains and balls to stand up in from of the state legislature and say, "We have the resources and space to build affordable housing outside of the city, away from the crack dealers and gang members, someplace where they don't bother anyone and no one bothers them. How can we get the space we need, the land where this can be built so EVERYONE can have a little breathing room, where EVERYONE can have a back yard to sit in the sun, where EVERYONE can have a barbecue and invite friends and neighbors?"

Skid Row may be a dumping ground for criminals and the mentally disabled, and honestly I am not unhappy that most of the state run inpatient facilities that were little more than prisons themselves have been shut down, but the condition in which the residents of Skid Row must survive is deplorable. The fact of the matter is that they can't take care of themselves and crowding them into a few city blocks only compounds the problems of mental health, hygiene, physical health, and addiction. Giving them a small income helps, yes, but it also is extremely damaging to someone trying to get clean.

Relying on GR and having cash that is not earned to spend is too easy of a way to keep the money going to the dope man and going through the endless cycle of jail, homelessness, jail, homelessness. Right when they get to the end of a thirty day clean, suddenly there is a new deposit of cash in the bank for them and they run out and get high for a few days and then the cycle keeps repeating itself.

Will Smith recently said in an interview, "All states should make it mandatory for drug tests to be given before welfare is approved". I disagree. I think the crime is that the reason that drugs are illegal in the first place is to keep a population under a very heavy hammer. The group at the top represent both sides, the drug pushers and the addicts. The addicts don't have any money so they make them into slave laborers for a few years in jail, while the ones who do have the money are let free on bail. The first anti-drug laws were created for police to go and raid Chinese opium dens because of widespread and only partially true stories circulating in tabloids about women having sex with the Chinese to supply their opium habits.

The people on Skid Row don't have an opium den to go to. They have no inner sanctum that allows them to escape the pressure of everyday life, and no matter where they go, someone else is there. Even if they have their own rooms or apartments the noise is so pervasive and non stop that it's impossible to ignore. Most solve the problem by turning their own music up even LOUDER, which again only makes it worse.

There is nowhere to quietly do homework, nowhere to be alone, focus, solve problems, and plan. The BLARING sirens of the Seventh Street Fire Station engines, the all night sirens of the 6th and Wall rampart police station (where the SWAT trucks and crew are located and drill at least twice a week with full sirens blaring from six trucks right through Skid Row in the middle of the night) is ABSOLUTELY meant to drive people insane! I understand why they built a major police station in the middle of the Skid Row ghetto. That was done so they could intimidate the poor and mentally unstable in the area even when they aren't arresting them or shaking them down on the street.

The downtown LAPD building between 5th and 6th on Wall street is one giant mess of people reporting crimes, homeless women crammed into the giant front entrances (they built this specifically so that anyone who wanted to could sleep under the safety blanket of the LAPD's webcams), never cleaned up piles of horse shit melting in the L.A. sun, and helicopters loudly taking off and landing every twenty minutes. Between all of that noise and the regular police business, there is the entire LAPD SWAT team, AR-15's loaded and ready twenty four hours a day seven days a week drilling twice a week with the sirens going full blast.

Tell me WHY we have to turn the sirens on at an ear piercing 220 dB when there is no emergency and it's three o'clock in the morning and there are ten thousand people sleeping in tents on the route we are going to take? Those people could use a good night's rest because the junkies kept them up all night screaming and the street cleaners will wake them up in ninety minutes at four thirty a.m. so running through the middle of their neighborhood with sirens on full blast is really going to piss some people off don't you think there are smarter ways to do this and win the hearts and minds of the people? Obviously, winning people over is not their intention. Obviously, making the police seem like your friend and protector is not their intention. Obviously, the poor being able to have a place to get their lives together and get clean from drugs and alcohol is not their intention.

CHAPTER TWENTY NINE

The worst is having an apartment when it rains and having to leave my friends outside. I know they would love to come upstairs and be warm and dry, but helping homeless people isn't as easy as it sounds. Almost every person I've had as a guest and who lives on the street (since getting in my apartment at 5th and San Pedro years later) has returned on my doorstep, unannounced, with a friend I've never seen before wanting to come in and use my bathroom and towels, asking for change, wanting to take a shower, trying to sell me a clock radio or some other such nonsense, and if you tell them you're too busy and not to knock at random times can be dangerous.

The homeless are so used to being turned away, rejected, vilified, told they are useless and chased out of stores and houses that they sometimes develop a 'red light' response to someone rejecting them. This can range from a barely perceptible scowl to full on war, and is unique to the person who is projecting it. However, it can be unnerving when they try to jam the door open and shove their way inside, so I keep a thick chain between the door and the wall so it will only open enough to talk to the person but not let them in.

Of course, everyone wants to see the recording studio I've built and hear the tracks I've done that they may have worked on, but often it's just an excuse to knock on the door at two a.m. Luckily the people I have invited up have all been musicians but they always want to bring a guest even when I ask them not to. Faced with a decision of recording with a great musician or turning them away and wondering if they're ever going to show up again, I almost always choose to do it as I may never get another chance.

These people must fight every day to protect what little they have. It is unfortunate that they must fight with each other for the smallest conveniences, socks, lighters, deodorant, even toothbrushes are stolen when your back is turned. My nickname while living in the 38th street shelter was 'the turtle' because I refused to take my backpack off ever. You wouldn't have either. The iPod and phone I had weren't worth much, but for a junkie needing a fix, they are solid gold.

Every afternoon in the park I'd listen to stories from the homeless who gathered there. I had a group of friends that consisted of a talkative but very sweet Rubanesque blonde girl who was on disability, a guy who was an AIDS patient and was growing thinner by the week, (he had good stories from his life in the state prison. My guess it was a mental institution, but I never press if they don't want to tell me). Another in our group was a Mexican Vietnam veteran who had been addicted to heroin since the Vietnam war, and his stories about scoring from the Viet Cong out in the jungle are also pretty amazing. We had a black guy who used to play bass on tour with some of the biggest funk bands in the world, and other colorful characters who would've easily made a day at the park in Skid Row a great reality show.

We sat in the park, smoked crack in the portable bathrooms, shot dope, and slept under the trees. Dinner was served in the mission about four o'clock. The food they served there was surprisingly good and you got a healthy portion. Baked chicken with mashed potatoes was common, Fridays they served fish, but all too often they served an unidentifiable brownish/ watery mess with old bread and very sugary water. It was served at breakfast, lunch and dinner at least a dozen times over the course of the week, but then the other mission served dinner at five o clock so if one failed to please, you could go to the next. The afternoons were the good times.

As soon as it got dark, it was dangerous. Light was fading when we got out of dinner and it was time to figure out our sleeping situation. I was still in the Panama, so I had no problem. My friend the AIDS patient was living in a tent right on fifth street. Everyone else had a plan for where to go, so we separated and went to our spots. I usually helped my friend set up his tent because he couldn't move very well. Every month he got about ninety oxycontins, (which are basically prescription heroin), and usually sold off fifty or so. It was important to get his tent set up early because as soon as it got dark, people came looking to rob, rape, kidnap, extort, and it was best not to be walking around unless you knew people and you knew the area.

The next morning, I got up at three thirty and hit the snooze. I woke up again at four, threw on some warm clothes, and walked to the area where the trucks came. It was about four thirty-one, and there wasn't a soul in sight. It was a very Twilight Zone-ish kind of quiet and I was wondering if it was a holiday or something. I asked a guy where everyone was and he told me they were all gone- the last truck left at four thirty. DAMN! ALL GONE?! SHIT! I knew there was no guarantee of getting work, but being late by showing up at four thirty?

That was too much. I had to make sure to be there at four. I went back to sleep. This was killing me. I got up at nine, got my shit together to go canning for the day, and hated my addiction even more.

CHAPTER THIRTY

What is addiction like? Why does it force peoples to survive like animals? I can't say exactly how it started for me, but that's not important. How it makes its way to people is different, but what happens to them is very similar physiologically. As you start to take the heroin, vicodin, morphine, opium, all derivatives of the poppy plant and all containing the same addictive chemical, you initially feel relaxed and even a bit sleepy, like you just had great sex, a great meal, or running a long distance. That's why it's so easy to get hooked on. You get the euphoria of something you did that was amazing and fulfilling, like kissing a girl for the first time that you had the biggest crush on or winning first place in a competition you had trained for years to win. You get to feel like you just won the lottery, and it only costs you your soul.

The opium (which is distilled into morphine base and then mixed with acidic anhydride in order to concentrate the morphine further into heroin) has the extremely peculiar quality of having molecules that fit exactly into the pleasure receptors of our brain (mu opioid receptors) in the Limbic System. The pleasure we naturally feel when we have a desirable experience like the ones listed above is triggered by a flood of endorphins and serotonin that fit into the same receptors. We normally get them when we are eating, or having sex, or after exercising, or feel pride, or love, or gamble, all of which are addictive.

Once the morphine is in the receptors your body sends a signal to stop sending (and eventually to stop manufacturing) these chemicals which are essential to you feeling good about yourself. Slowly over time they stop growing completely as you use more and more opiates to get the same effect. This is when you're an addict. You're using the drug no longer just to get high, but to cure the pain of withdrawal. As soon as you stop taking the opiate filled drugs, there are no natural chemicals left to fill the pleasure activating mu opioid receptors in your brain, and your body goes into a panic mode.

I've read that the brain has the same reaction withdrawing from heroin as it does when it senses the body is on fire, which I can vouch for being accurate. It is a HORRIBLE, vicious, mind numbing pain I have had to live in fear of for years, and nothing will take the pain away except for another hit of heroin. The withdrawal creeps up on you like the setting sun, you know it is coming, it is always coming, and until you get clean, it is always following you.

When you get your first hit of the day, that monster is so far away you can't even remember it exists. As the hours creep on and you fail to come up with either dope or cash, the first shadows start to fall on buildings miles away from you, but you can still see them. You feel the ground tremor from its footsteps, still far enough away to be in motion at full speed but if you run you had better run wisely and use your resources in the best way possible otherwise you're going down fast.

Another four hours go by. You make phone calls, think of ways to get out of work, think of ways to get cash. You're still active and have a few possibilities, so you're not in any danger. Not yet, anyway.

After from eight to sixteen hours, you start to feel sick.

It's a chill at first, a slight sweat that gathers on your upper lip and forehead, but you still have time. You look around and decide to leave whatever the hell you're doing in order to score as quickly as possible. Your regular plans to connect with the drugs have fallen through. Someone took off with the money and never returned, your regular dealer got busted, the shit you went over the bridge for was fake, the script you had lined up was discovered by the pharmacy, one way or another you keep trying to make it happen, but you need to realize the dope is not coming.

Your body goes into panic mode as you go through all the motions of trying to score. Cash money, dealers, gangsters, hookers, dark alleyways, cheap hotel rooms, government subsidized apartments, shit filled back streets, tent cities, ghettos and housing projects, needles, cookers, ties, blood, these things become more familiar as you get to know more junkies and you need them to score. They will need you as well. It is best to keep your options open and your phone turned on, otherwise, you'll never be able to find dope.

The pain is growing now. It's cramping your legs badly, you feel sluggish and heavy as it slowly takes over your body. Your nose begins to run and your stomach feels all fucked up as the waste in your system begins to turn into water. Soon you're shitting in dark alleyways too. The unstoppable diarrhea means you certainly aren't going to make it home to your own bathroom and restaurants will not even let you in the door. You've got no choice as the contents of your lower intestine are now just water and if you don't let it out you will shit all over yourself.

It will come at the least opportune moment. My most horrible nightmare came true as I had to borrow a Ziploc baggie on a crowded public train to relieve myself into.

It was rush hour.

It smelled awful. I apologized profusely.

If you become an addict, moments like this will become a reality. Don't do it. Just walk away.

I was extremely appreciative of the people who did no more than perhaps raise a cloth over their faces and looked at me in pity. For once in my life I deserved it.

CHAPTER THIRTY ONE

Twenty to twenty four hours without heroin, that's when the REAL fun starts. The sickness will not go away. It will get worse, much worse, and now you have double vision and can hardly focus long enough to cross the street. My vision has been so bad that I felt in danger for my life several times trying to simply cross at a red light. You are now sweating profusely, most likely vomiting whatever may have been in your stomach and in severe pain from the hurls and muscle cramps which take over every limb in your body. The symptoms are different for everyone as everyone's body chemistry is different, but I have yet to meet a person who suffers no discomfort.

In most cases, it is severe enough to do things that you would never consider doing before like stealing from your parents, lying to your girlfriend, dipping into your children's college fund, using your rent to buy drugs.

In more extreme cases, you do things that other people dictate that you do or they will withhold drugs and money from you. This is how pimps are able to keep a stranglehold on prostitutes, by getting them addicted to heroin. They are so terrified of the pain of withdrawal that they are willing to debase and degrade themselves to the point of absolute submission in order to stop the pain of withdrawal. It feels like there is a fire burning inside your skin, and it goes on and on and on for days and you suffer and want to die.

Once you hit the twenty-four-hour mark, you're in really bad shape. You're in so much pain you'd steal the $5 from your own kids if you had to, no matter what your principles are. I consider myself a strong person, but I had no idea what I was up against when I started, and no idea how long it was going to last. After twenty-four hours, unless you are planning on getting clean, pretty much everything you do and say will be to get dope or money for it. Your body is a shaking stinking mess of sweat and shit and urine, some are on your clothes and you are seriously on your way to an early grave.

If you have never tried an opiate, unless you are in SEVERE pain, I highly suggest you never do. They are much too easily available these days. I have had many friends who, upon trying heroin, were simply ill all night, and thought it was a horrible experience, never to try it again.

How I envy them.

I wish I had been told how severe the addiction is, and how intense the pain is when you are trying to kick. It is absolutely the worst feeling in the world and I was completely unprepared. As I got sicker and sicker and finally at a point where I was out of cash, out of friends, out of things I could pawn or sell, out of options, out of a home, and out of luck, that's when the real pain hit.

You can't sleep during withdrawal. No way. Night time is an unending hell, your muscles cramp and twitch all night, forcing you to bend and flex them constantly, which gave rise to the saying, "Kick the habit". You vomit anything that is in your stomach and sweat profusely as you try in vain to get comfortable.

The pain is unbearable.

Your entire body shivers and my balls would ache as if someone had kicked them so hard that they recessed back up into my body and stayed there like two pissed off turtles.

Little things can be helpful, cigarettes, alcohol, I would drink an entire fifth of Black Velvet whiskey on nights that I couldn't score and had the extra cash. Being that drunk in a city like Los Angeles is extremely dangerous. I was totally out of control and there looked to be no way out. I tried to kick, I really did, but it takes six weeks to get clean (and even then it's always going to be an issue for you) and I only had the hotel for another four or five days. It was a horrible, horrible experience.

I had lost everything, everything I had in the world that was valuable was gone and was not coming back. I was on the street and in severe pain. The shock to your system when you finally have no place to go is truly horrible. You have no bathroom, no privacy, and everywhere you go in the city people look at you like you're a piece of trash. I smelled awful and water coming out of a shower felt like razor blades cutting through my skin so I started to look and smell really bad. My clothes soaked up the sweat and dried, leaving a residue and making them look more and more like rags every day.

I was becoming one of the undead, one of the faceless, nameless people who we see walking around every day and we ignore as best we can. In groups, in front of other people, we try as hard as we can to show compassion and understanding, but in reality we wish for a place they could all get help in peace. I had such a promising start in life, good grades at university, a great job, and finally a record contract in Hollywood. Now, I was lurking around the filthy sections of Los Angeles digging through trash just to stay well another day. It was a non stop hell. I had no choice; the pain was too intense.

I considered suicide daily.

CHAPTER THIRTY TWO

Now I was sick, but I didn't have a dime to my name. I walked up and down the street, looking for anyone I knew who might be able to help me out. No luck. I was sitting on the side of the street, asking, praying, how the hell was I going to get my hands on a couple of dollars? There's got to be a way.

The reason I love Los Angeles is because she always takes care of me, and I always seem to find a bed, food, dope, or money right when I need to. This guy I'd never seen before walks up to me and says,

"Hey, do you know where to get any dope?"

I jumped right up.

"Yeah, uhh, YEAH! I can hook you up, but you gotta kick me down a bag, ok?"

"Shit, man you get me six and get two for yourself, okay?"

"YOU'RE ON!!!"

Within five minutes I had two bags of dope in my hands and eternal gratitude to whoever was looking out for me. I loved Los Angeles. I was never hungry, sick, tired, dirty, or bored for very long. There was always someone there for me, and I always tried to return the favor when the situation presented itself. I flew to my room, fixed, lay down on my bed and slept until early the next morning.

The next day after work I went to the needle exchange. This was in a little storefront right near Skid Row. They provided all kinds of services- They offered clean needles for anyone who wanted them, sponsored a heroin anonymous meeting every Thursday, and had a doctor every Tuesday who would look at your ailments for free and could usually treat them. This was mostly for abscesses, giant skin lesions that popped up from shooting with infected needles, shooting in dirty areas, or if you missed your vein and got the dope under your skin. These were particularly nasty boils that grew to the size of a silver dollar and were extremely painful as they were, but if you tried to pop one by yourself it was nothing short of excruciating.

It was not uncommon to see the homeless performing a kind of street surgery on these- I saw a woman getting lanced by her friend on the street to try and relieve some of the pressure from one of these infections, and then they tried squeezing out the infected pus. It was horrific- she was screaming in pain, and eventually a black ball of poison popped out from under her skin. She had obviously done this many times, because she had little quarter sized scars all up and down her arms.

This was why it was so important to me to always keep and use clean needles. I am eternally grateful to the needle exchange for the service they provided, because people who are desperate to get dope in their system will use any needle available- ones found on the street, in the garbage, or they'll just use one from anyone they ask. I never EVER shared a needle in the whole time I ever shot dope, but there are so many who just don't care about themselves at all. Whether due to abuse, ennui, entitlement, injury, disease, age, fraud, or whatever, Skid Row is heavily populated with the most depressed and isolated people in the world, all bunched together and living in an urban hell, and heroin and crack provide the smallest relief from their worst enemy, themselves.

The needle exchange is the concentration of the lowest and the worst off, because not only are they homeless and unable to care for themselves, but they have the additional burden of drug addiction, and it is RAMPANT in Skid Row. Drugs are so easily available there that even though I live one block from the convenience store, on the way there and back I am offered pills, heroin, crack, speed, and about everything else.

They even give you a card at the needle exchange saying you can legally carry needles on your person- a cop can still search you or detain you for it, but they provide free legal service for anyone who gets arrested for a needle as paraphernalia. The government wants people to have access to clean needles to prevent the spread of aids.

Inspiration hit like a bolt of lightning.

CHAPTER THIRTY THREE

Why not make needles available to people when buying dope?

I was off and running.

I got to the needle exchange and got about twenty needles. They give you five extra plus one for every needle you bring in. I had fifteen, so I took them and headed down to the dope spot. I just followed one of the dealers until he made a sale and then asked the guy, "You need any outfits?" He didn't even think about it and pulled out two dollars. "YEAH! Lemme get two." Within ten minutes I made five dollars- enough for one hit.

Within an hour I had sold all twenty except one for myself. This was a blessing- going from having to walk for eight to ten hours digging through trash, to walking from 5 a.m. to noon non- stop carrying a fifty-pound bag full of flyers just to make what I could make in two hours standing comfortably on the street selling clean needles. The problem was that you needed needles to exchange in order to get them. I only had one, but where there's a problem, there's a solution.

There was more than one needle exchange. The one downtown was only open Mondays and Wednesday mornings. If you missed it, there was one at a stop for the homeless called the Hippie Kitchen. This was a little garden area in the middle of Skid Row that had a needle exchange, gave free food to the homeless, provided fresh cold water, and was a nice peaceful place to sit and play chess or read a book. It was a pretty little garden that had a koi pond, a waterfall, lots of trees and plants, and funky hippie people in charge of it.

There was also a needle exchange on the outskirts of McArthur park, two subway stops away that was open Thursday nights out of a van that pulled up next to the Home Depot on Birmingham, and there was ANOTHER one that was open Thursday and Sunday nights of f of LaBrea and Santa Monica in Hollywood.

The needle exchange that was in Hollywood sold boxes of 100 needles for a donation of $10, and that was a couple of days away, so I knew I was going to have to hustle a few more days to keep my money together and buy a few hundred needles. Soon I bought two boxes full and sold them out in three days. The police saw what I was doing and let me walk on by. They wanted junkies to use clean needles, mostly because they got poked as well when going through clothes and searching the addicts. One of the first things a police officer will ask you before searching you is, "Do you have any sharp objects on you, anything that will poke me or tear a hole in my gloves?" Having clean needles on the street protected them as well.

Over the years I would get to know the needle exchange people well. The people who use their time to provide this service are some of the best people I have ever come across while in the depths of addiction. Never judgmental or condescending, they are mostly ex- addicts themselves or health care specialists who are way too low paid. There is a bag lunch for anyone who is hungry, and the people who get your information (initials, they keep it anonymous) are especially courteous. They seem to understand that addicts are going through an extremely difficult time in their lives and seem to genuinely want to be there to help.

There is always a small crowd when they open the doors, but you can be in and out in five minutes. No long lines or processing, you simply show them how many you brought and they exchange them for fresh ones. A large metal collection safety can sits in the middle of the room and people scoop their dirty needles into it, turn around, and get a paper bag filled with sterile water, cookers, alcohol pads to prevent infection, condoms, rubber ties to tie off your vein, and fresh needles.

The needle exchanges employed some of the most colorful people I have ever met. One of the clinicians showed a film in the lobby about his time in Indonesia. He bought a boat to motor to Australia, got stranded in the middle of the ocean, and had to be saved by a Russian trawler. One of the needle exchange guys on Sunset boulevard used to play guitar for Christian Death. A girl at the Skid Row clinic was actor Danny Trejo's sister and was always pleasant to talk to. Having someone be friendly to you in a world that sees you as the enemy has a very strong effect on you. You can see that even though you don't believe in yourself and think there is no way out of your situation, there is someone in the world who does believe in you.

CHAPTER THIRTY FOUR

It's amazing the variety of entrepreneurial skill and hustle you see going on amongst the homeless. Some of them are so ingenious that if some of these people were working in the private sector they would be millionaires by now. They apply such dedication and precision to their hustle that it is amazing that they ever lost their way and wound up down here. This only goes to prove that it could happen to anyone.

There were college graduates, ex- models, ex- stock brokers, ex- professional athletes. You hit a streak of bad luck, invest everything you've got into trying to get yourself out, wind up deeper in debt or trouble, and before you know it you're out of friends, out of a place to stay, out of money, and out of luck.

Some people here were just too proud to let others who would have helped them know they were in such dire circumstances. Some didn't want their families to know they were addicted to drugs or alcohol and wanted to stay down here where they were easily accessible. Then there were those who were just plain fuck ups and had as much bad street credibility as they probably had bad reputations in the rest of the other world.

Not everyone here was just down on their luck. There were those who were born poor, failed to get an education, and/ or never developed enough skills to get and keep a job. People like this were in abundance down here and those were the ones who felt that this was THEIR world and people like me were just visiting. In a manner of speaking, they were right.

For some people, this was their PERMANENT home, and for someone like me to come in and talk about how shitty it was and how great life was anyplace OTHER than here must have induced bitterness that I perceived as racism. Either way, I had just as much right to use the services provided by the state or a church as they did.

The attitude some of these people displayed ranged from disrespectful to violent. I saw a van pulled over on the street around the corner from the Midnight Mission. It was a Korean Christian Church, and several of its members had pulled together a van load of sandwiches, doughnuts, and iced tea to give out to whoever wanted food. A man at the front took one look at the baloney sandwich he was handed, threw it down on the ground in front of the people who were nice enough to give it to him, and yelled, "Man, what is this shit?? BALONEY SANDWICHES?!?! You Chi- nese got more money that! Come back here when you got some REAL food!!" He then wrapped up a doughnut with a napkin, took an iced tea, and left the sandwich there on the ground.

The poor girl who had just given it to him was so shocked and scared that she started to cry. Others came up to her position, comforted her, and walked her to sit in the passenger side of the van. I was ashamed for him. That man was so rude to someone who was just trying to be nice that it put a black cloud over the whole congregation.

This was a common reaction to people giving out free food and drinks here. If it wasn't good enough for someone they were sure to verbalize it, and that was such a disgusting display of selfishness that it had to disappoint the people giving the food out. Several times whole TRUCKS would pull up with crates of little drink boxes, tortilla chips, different kinds of candy, soup mixes, maybe even bread or milk, and sometimes boxes of cereal. Boxes were flying everywhere as the homeless grabbed as much of the good stuff for themselves as they could. Arms and cardboard flew everywhere and fights often broke out.

The people handing things out would try to keep order, but if there was something in demand like pudding cups, which could be sold on the street for fifty cents, they were shoved out of the way as people filled their backpacks and duffel bags with as much of it as they could. The homeless would even carry off the wood pallets at the bottom of the piles which they could sell to the pallet yard that was half a mile south of downtown. I've seen guys steal pallets from up by the Denny's on Figueroa, and then walk two miles with a pallet under each arm- these things weighed fifteen pounds each and would riddle your arm with splinters. The price you got for them was about $2.25.

Another time I knew an older Latino guy who seemed to be followed around daily by this white man who was a bit younger. The older man could not get around very well and was constantly being tended to by the other man. I wondered why the other man just didn't take on an easier person or thought they were dealing dope together, but later that week I walked by their tent and saw them wrapped up in a little ball together, fast asleep in each other's arms. It's encouraging to see a little bit of love in a place that you never thought it existed.

CHAPTER THIRTY FIVE

After getting a flow for buying and selling clean needles on the street, I was actually making some money and could afford to get what I wanted to eat for breakfast. In the early morning there was a coffee and doughnut shop that opened on 5th street just east of Broadway. They had the most AMAZING doughnuts for fifty cents, and it was breakfast every morning. They were giant cakes about six inches in diameter still soft and warm from the oven. They had a layer of chocolate fudge dripping over the tops that was nothing short of delectable, and one of these giants would fill you up. It was often a hard choice for me whether to get my morning hit right then or wait another ten minutes because I HAD to have one of these doughnuts. It was not your average pastry. It was sinful. That and an over sugared cup of coffee was perfection on a chilly winter morning.

I was about to run out of time at the Panama. My two weeks were up, and I had to decide what to do. I ran over to the midnight mission to see about getting a bed, but they were full. The Los Angeles Mission had beds available, but you had to be at the mission at 5 pm. to get your bed every night. Plus, they had kind of a bad reputation as far as racism goes, so whites were generally given a bad time when they were in there. Blacks would harass white guys so that beds would be available for their buddies, and it went far beyond verbal taunting.

I did a bit of research, asked around, and came up with what I thought was the perfect solution. If you were on General Relief, which I was, you were qualified for a place to live at the House of Hope. The House of Hope was a state subsidized housing project where you were given a bed in a room with five other guys, breakfast, lunch, and dinner, and you could come and go as you pleased. It was located on Pico and Western which was ten minute walk, so the location was ideal. They didn't search you or drug test you, even though the state requirements said you were supposed to, and everyone I knew said it was a cool place if you could get in there.

I figured the cost of meals alone was worth the price. How it was paid for was you gave them your General Relief card which was like an ATM card and the pin number, and they withdrew the money every month from your account and the state paid the rest. It was supposed to be kind of a halfway house with drug counseling and prayer sessions for parolees and the like, but really it was a money making scam for the guys who ran it. The put six to eight guys to a room and there were about ten rooms in the house. Sixty guys paying $220 a month each comes to $13,000 in rent paid to them every month. That house couldn't have been worth more than $1700 every month. The linoleum was peeling from the floor, the pipes were clogged and brown rust came in with the water. For the time being, I had no choice.

CHAPTER THIRTY SIX

Early mornings were peaceful on Skid Row. There were a lot of people up and around who had been kicked out of their beds at the missions and dealers were never far from the scene, but they were still groggy and mostly sat around the street or waited in line for breakfast somewhere. I hit the street between six and seven a.m. when there was the most drug traffic. The stores weren't open yet and people would drive up to get their dope before work that day. There was a lot of traffic during the day, but that was all from out of work junkies, and the good dealers were gone by ten a.m.

As soon as I hit the street, I walked around going "outfits! outfits!" and connecting people with a dealer in exchange for a buck or two. It never took more than a half an hour to get my five bucks. Then I got my first balloon for the day, sat down in Pershing Square park, and cooked up my breakfast hit. Pershing Square was a quiet little oasis in the middle of downtown. It was about a city block in size, not a lot of forested area, but just enough trees and shrubs for ideal hiding spots to hit up in.

After getting my morning fix, I sat in the garden area by the fountain and felt the morphine flow through my body. Sometimes I fell asleep sitting there. It had such a Zen like feel to it that it made relaxation in a chaotic situation a welcome endeavor. Squirrels and pigeons chattered noisily as the cleanup crew sprayed the sidewalks with hoses, and junkies, crack heads, and homeless people leaned on the concrete benches for a moment of solitude before the day started.

Once in a while you'd see a junkie pulling water into his syringe from the fountain. That water was filthy, I mean, pigeons shit in there, you know? I would always opt to spend the extra dollar to get a clean bottle of water, and if you didn't have a dollar, you could run into the Subway sandwich shop and grab a few ice cubes. You really didn't need that much water, and that fountain was gross.

Another interesting thing about living on Skid Row are the allegiances you make. In the real world you make allegiances based on business and social needs. On Skid Row you make allegiances based on immediate gratification. If you needed to get hooked up with dope and someone had a connection, away you went. If you needed a spot to crash and had a few extra bucks or some dope, it was never hard to find what you needed.

I helped out a guy who was so fucked up on pills he couldn't see straight, but he needed to get to Santa Monica an hour away by bus to pick up a check. He offered to pay me twenty bucks to get him there and back safely, and twenty would do me fine, so away we went. I earned that twenty, though. He was such a mess I had to literally pick him up and put him on the bus at every stop, walk him through the process at the check cashing station, and fight for my twenty bucks because then he didn't want to give it to me.

I hung out with crack heads, transvestite hookers, pimps, paroled murderers, rich kids from Beverly Hills, rock stars, movie stars, there was such a wide variety of junkies that it would've made a great sitcom. One of my friends from the street was a drag queen/ princess. She was one of the types who knew EVERYONE on the street and was constantly saying hello to people as we walked along looking for our favorite dealers. The great thing about drag queens is that they are always fun to hang out with and always know the best dealers, what's happening on the street, and which cops to watch out for.

I was WAY on the other side of the city from where I kept my bedroll stashed by the freeway, and it was too late to go back to the house, so she offered to let me fix at her place in exchange for a hit.

I accepted, and we walked, and walked, and walked for about an HOUR. This might seem like a long distance, but she was wearing heels and wobbling uncomfortably in them. I was getting pissed, and she kept going, "Oh, it's just another few blocks, we're almost there". Another few blocks later, and she'd say "I'm sorry, it's a little farther than I thought." We were in the industrial area, down by Alameda and Olympic, far away from where anyone else was on a REALLY dark street.

"Here we are!"

"Where, in this building?"

"No, I sleep right here, help me find some boxes."

She slept on the street under a light post, in a filthy doorway under an awning that kept her dry in the rain. It was very sad but I was in no mood to be sympathetic.

"WHAT? You just walked me a mile to sleep in a DOORWAY on the STREET?! !!"

"Well, I'm SORRY but this is all I've got!"

"Yeah but you should've TOLD we were gonna have to sleep on the STREET! You said you had a PLACE and THAT'S why we've been walking all the way OUT here!"

"Well, when I said my place I MEANT my spot on the street. I'm sorry, do you want to go back to your spot?"

"Shit, it's two miles back the other way! I'm NOT giving you a hit to sleep on the fucking STREET."

"WHAT?!?! YOU PROMISED ME!"

"YEAH BUT YOU SAID YOU HAD A PLACE WE COULD STAY!!"

"PLEASE DON'T DO THIS TO ME! I'LL PAY YOU BACK TOMORROW I SWEAR!"

"You KNEW I thought you had an apartment or room. No way. You walked me ALL this way just to sleep in a BOX on the STREET. FORGET IT."

She started to cry. She begged me for a hit, and I KNEW she was going to be sick, but there was no way I was giving up a hit of dope for this. I could sleep on the street ANYWHERE. This was just one example of the kind of fucked up shit that goes on down here.

I wound up crashing there, mostly because it was cold out and I didn't want to walk back for half an hour in the night air. What I didn't realize was that I would wake up in the middle of the night barely covered in half of a ragged, hole ridden blanket. I decided to do a hit of dope to keep off the chill, and that set my friend in a tantrum.

She was DESPERATE for a hit, and that's why she dragged me all the way out here and it was TORTURE watching me cook up and hit. I would have done it anyway, but I was angry at her for deceiving me like that. She KNEW I was going to be upset, but she figured I would at least throw her down a balloon until morning when she would pay me back.

I knew loaning a homeless junkie was pretty much just giving it away and in other circumstances I might have done it just to be a nice guy, but this was deliberate and scandalous so she got left out. About five thirty a.m. the street cleaners came by and told us to move, so while still shaking from the chills, I got up and walked all the way back to my other spot by the freeway. I did up the rest of the dope and fell asleep, happy to have saved the hit for myself.

.

CHAPTER THIRTY SEVEN

Living in poverty is a constant lesson in humiliation. There was no privacy except for the few minutes in the bathroom you got until someone started banging on the door. I thought this would be the ideal place to live, but this asshole director was making it a living hell. All I knew was that I had to get out of there. Living in the Missions was better than this. At least there I didn't have some asshole singling me out to take his aggressions out on and I didn't feel like there was a racist edge to everything that went on around me.

In the meantime, I had plenty of needles to get me the money I needed for dope, food, and whatever else I wanted. It wasn't going to get me off the street, but at least I didn't have to do anything like dig through trash cans or get chased out of a neighborhood by a guy with his dogs. There were plenty of chicken hawks working the streets as well, and they didn't hesitate to come up to the young white boys like me and offer us work.

I knew more than a few kids who were hustlers, prostitutes, sex workers, all of them addicts. Almost all of them had stories of being raped by fathers and brothers, lied to by boyfriends and husbands and turned out to have sex with strangers to keep the pimp boyfriend in heroin or crack. I couldn't help but want to give them a place to go, somewhere that they didn't have to feel ashamed to be themselves.

In groups or on the street, they looked a bit nicer than the street junkies like me who hustled needles and pills and dope, because most of them made enough to keep an apartment or hotel room. We silently allowed them their excuses on why they had so much cash on them daily.

My tax refund came in.

I worked my ass off at the restaurant last night.

This one guy tipped me a hundred bucks.

They never spoke of the work that they did and we never asked. They were good looking enough that people wanted to pay them for sex, and we weren't. I certainly would have been a very charming gigolo, and we all like to think of ourselves as desirable but my too thin butt and pirate's teeth made me more of an object of affection for punk rock girls and bleeding hearts rather than pretty junkie girls who always had rich boyfriends. If you were dirty, overweight, and mean, no one was going to pay you for sex. That's not entirely true, you can always get paid for sex no matter what you look or act like, but it is going to be far from comfortable living.

The street addicts were the junkies no one wanted to help, no one wanted to touch, there was no redeeming quality of unselfishness left in them. The women I see out on the streets, ragged, abused, half way to their graves so far down the scale all they care about is getting another hit of crack so they can escape from the nightmare of their lives for two minutes more than anyone need a place to go, a place they can be safe from men, from coercion, from rape, from sex slavery, from drug addiction, and the shelters the state and churches supply are very poorly funded.

Their stories were the most tragic of all. They were the ones who didn't care what happened to them because no one else cared about them. Many of them have been on their own since they were young, had parents that were abusive, were in foster care, and had been rejected by everyone they grew up around. I couldn't figure out if they were antisocial because they had been rejected by everyone, or if they had been rejected by everyone because they were antisocial. They learned that in order to survive without being someone's sex slave they had to have no shame, no morals, and no connections with anyone.

CHAPTER THIRTY EIGHT

After a month or two straight of working the street, you saw the same people every day doing their same hustle. They all wound up on 5th and Broadway at some point and I was getting to know a large circle of regulars. Once in a while one of these people wouldn't show up for a few days, and if it was one of the daily crew, rumors started flying. The first rumor that flew around was that they were picked up by the police. If they got busted you usually heard about it from someone who got out of jail.

Every day someone would get back on the street and they would report on who was incarcerated. The gang kept close tabs on which of their sales people got arrested, and if they were high up enough would bail them out. They needed replacements for the youngsters they left in jail, and there were more than enough illegal residents to fill their shoes. Some of these were kids who wanted to join the gang, some just needed to make money, but the position of dealer was greatly coveted by both immigrant gangsters and the homeless.

There were actually two positions the gang had. One was the regular street dealer, who bought packets of twelve balloons for forty dollars. Each balloon sold for five bucks, so you made twenty dollars on each pack. Those packs went fast though, and often were sold out as soon as the dealer hit the street. A good dealer could go through fifteen packs in a day, so there was some decent money to be made. The homeless were scraping up five bucks for their one balloon, but the kids who drove in from Hollywood or the valley picked up ten or twenty balloons at a time.

The other position was to be the paquetero, or pack man. The pack man held all of the balloons to give to the dealers. He was given ten plastic bags with twelve packs each in them, each pack containing twelve balloons and collected the money from each dealer. Since each pack sold for forty dollars, they were holding about forty-eight hundred dollars when they sold the last of the packs. They were closely followed by about three or four gang members so they wouldn't bail with the money but also so they wouldn't get robbed by anyone with enough balls to try and do it. If they didn't have some shooters hovering nearby them, they would've been jumped.

If you got caught with that much dope you would get three years, minimum. They were less inclined to get their own guys put away for that long, so they recruited one of the homeless guys they knew to do it. The job paid three hundred dollars for the day, but I knew two guys who did it and they both got ripped off. At the end of the day, the gang members told them they were short on money and they were going to take it out of the cash they were getting paid. One of the guys

I knew wasn't a thief, he worked all day and didn't get paid anything.

The other guy I knew, Ira, was questionable, and he said he didn't get paid either but I wouldn't have been surprised if he actually DID take the money. They told me they re-upped their load six or seven times during the day. That's eight hundred and forty packs of dope, or ten thousand and eighty balloons, street price, fifty thousand, four hundred dollars, seven days a week, three hundred sixty-five days a year. That's some serious dope.

Tre, the leader of the morning crew, came up to me looking VERY pissed off.

"YOU SEEN IRA?!?!"

"Not since this morning, why?"

"NOBODY'S SEEN HIM. IF YOU SEE HIM, TELL HIM TO CALL ME!"

I knew what had happened. Ira waited until he had about two or three thousand dollars in cash and took the rest of the dope and bailed. This meant there would be no more dope on the street for the next three hours while the gang looked for him, figured he was either busted or bailed, found another paquetero, and resupplied the street with dope. This ALSO meant there would be fifty to a hundred junkies walking around the block, all shaking their heads whenever they passed one another.

CHAPTER THIRTY NINE

Broadway is a tragic comedy when there's no dope to be found. A hundred junkies walk around in a circle, most of them semi- familiar with each other. Two people will be on the pay phone with another five people hovering close by hoping whoever is on the other end will connect them. Others will be rounding up people to go down to the tent cities on San Julian and Gladys. No one likes going there alone Your chances of getting ripped off are high down there, plus that part of town is run by the black gangs, so it's unnerving for whites to go by themselves. The rest of the junkies will just sit on the corner on 6th and Spring just around the corner from the main dealing area. When a dealer is re-upped with supply, that's the direction they come from so whoever is near that corner will get served first, if at all.

If a dealer DOES show up, he'll get MOBBED by the people waiting there. Everyone wants to get served before he runs out, so fistfights often break out over who was in line first, and it's every man for himself. I've had dealers who were friends of mine show up with a few packs, and I'll let them know I'm there and they'll signal they'll save me some, only to get one hit if any when he gets to me. I hate rushing into the mob scene. It makes it too obvious for the police to know what's going on, but it's either that or go without and wait for the next guy.

The guys who keep order in these situations are the enforcers. These are the soldiers that you never see walking the street close by, but they're at the end of the block and tell people to chill out, walk slow, and everyone listens. They're usually in a SUV that sits in one of the parking lots controlled by the gang. I've seen two girls who were dealing for the gang get ripped off and the guy was stupid enough to stick around, taunting them into a fight. One of the girls dialed a number and within forty seconds an SUV came tearing around the corner, and six gang members jumped out and just PUMMELED the guy into unconsciousness. They rifled through his pockets, got their money back, and left him bleeding in the middle of the street.

It was over in about thirty seconds. Once they jumped out and identified him, it was like a swarm of angry bees- they blasted him with repeated punches to the head, and once he was down they kicked him repeatedly as hard as they could on the concrete. Even as he lay still and unconscious, he was beaten to the point where I thought he was going to get killed. The enforcers jumped back into the SUV with the girls and took off.

The police arrived five minutes later. By that time a crowd had gathered around the guy who was slowly coming to. The cops got him on his feet, asked him a few questions and let him stumble on his way. Having seen him taunt those girls like he was some big shot gangster, he really was asking for it. When there's fifty thousand dollars floating around this street every day, you can bet a big part of that cash goes toward the enforcers. It's rare for people to rip off the gang not only for fear of retribution, but because you've got to come back the next day to score and if no one trusts you, you'll go without and that's way worse.

Once someone is blacklisted by the gang, their only hope is to have someone else score for them, and that'll cost. This is how they keep everyone in line. It's also how I made some extra money. I was one of the only people on the street to have a cell phone, so giving my number out to junkies who needed to be hooked up always meant I would get paid something in return, and I ALWAYS needed dope. The other thing is that scenes like this bring the police, and when patrol cars show up, the entire operation shuts down for an hour or two, so NOBODY gets to score. Then you've got junkies walking the streets again, and more and more come as time goes by until they finally get the dealers back on the streets.

I've seen it take two days. They were so pissed off at the junkies and addicts that they withheld all the dope in Los Angeles, and there wasn't a bag or balloon to be found anywhere in town. The addicts were about to tear open the methadone clinic and take everything that was in there, and everyone walked the streets in an endless circle of despair. It was a nightmare.

CHAPTER FORTY

There were occasional busts, but they were few and far between. Once every two weeks the cops would swarm down on 6th street at six thirty in the morning and line everyone up, search them, and move on their way. The lookouts on either end of the block would yell, "ONE TIME!" and everyone would stash their dope in garbage cans, sewer drains, doorway jams, or just stash it in their pants. Everyone was lined up along the wall, hands behind their backs, and if anyone was unlucky enough to have any dope in their pockets they got busted for possession and taken to county.

Most of the dealers and junkies kept the dope in their mouths so if they got searched they just swallowed it. You could usually fit about twelve balloons in your mouth but trying to swallow that many isn't as easy as it sounds. I had to swallow FOUR once and I almost choked. After the cops left, everyone grabbed water bottles, went into the park, and spent the next twenty minutes trying to barf up the balloons they had just swallowed.

It was pretty funny seeing all these gangsters sticking their fingers down their throats, chugging water and picking through their vomit. Some even stood on their heads to try and get the balloons to sink to the top of their stomachs. It seemed like the police had a certain amount of tolerance for all of this activity. It was done so brazenly in the open that everyone wanted to get in on the action. Out of twenty or so dealers that walked the streets daily, maybe one would get busted every week. A lot more were shaken down, taken to the station and questioned, or just extorted for their money, but it seemed the risk was low at this time so everyone wanted to be in on it.

The cops already knew I was the needle guy. The first time they shook me down I was walking along Broadway. I didn't have any dope on me but I had a crack pipe in my pocket. I wasn't a crack smoker, but sometimes I would wake up with a raging headache and crack seemed to clear it up in an instant, so once in a while I took a hit. The patrol car was cruising in the other direction, so they passed right by me and I saw out of the corner of my eye that they were watching me. They pulled over and got out, and in the reflection of a glass shop door I saw them coming towards me. I quickly turned the corner and WHIPPED that crack pipe under a car.

The reason I'll never buy a Pyrex pipe is because they're harder to break. Most crack smokers swear by them, but when I threw that regular glass pipe it busted into about a million pieces and totally disintegrated. The cops sure enough ran right up behind me, grabbed my hands and cuffed me against the wall.

"What ja throw?"

"Nothing."

"You saw us comin' boy, you were scared!"

His partner was shining his flashlight where I threw the pipe but there wasn't enough left of it to gather as evidence. The guy searching me found a hundred wrapped up brand new needles, but no dope.

"So, you're the needle guy, huh?"

I already had an answer well prepared.

"Well, the way I see it is that I provide a much needed community service. If clean needles are available, it keeps the number of aids cases down. Every AIDS case costs the state approximately eighty thousand dollars annually in taxpayer money for medical care, drugs, and hospice beds. I keep the number of new AIDS cases to a minimum"

They were both laughing at this point, I've used that speech before and it has just the right balance of comedy and bullshit to keep them from pushing it any further.

"Okay buddy, take your needles and get out of here, but don't let me catch you with any dope, or I'll take you right in, you got it?"

I got it.

CHAPTER FORTY ONE

I had seen how a lot of other people out on the street lived. Compared to their situations, my spot was a palace. There were the people who lived in doorways on cardboard boxes on Broadway, but there was so much activity going on all night I couldn't believe that they ever got any sleep at all. This is another factor that adds to the psychosis of the already disturbed waters of the homeless mind.

Further down were the missions, and the overflow from those spilled out into the street right in front of them. The last chance for a bed was at the Midnight mission at around eleven o'clock, but there was usually a line for those and if you weren't in line by nine p.m., you usually didn't get a cot. They let people sleep in the foyer entranceway to the mission that held about a hundred and fifty people. It was crowded, too bright, noisy, and you had to sleep on concrete, but it was safety from the streets.

Behind the missions on Gladys and Towne streets were the tent cities. Crack dealers, prostitutes, thieves, gangsters, anyone who had business late at night usually stayed down here. This was the area that was more territorial. There was a Cuban section, a Northerners and Southerners area, the Africans and the gays all had their own place, and it was a really grim place to visit.

People urinated and defecated in the street, so it smelled like rotten feces everywhere you went. The fish warehouse markets close by added to that stench, so only the most disturbed and desperate would stay in the area. Women would just pull up their skirts, pull down their underwear and let fly, so you had to watch where you stepped. This was one of the areas the city will just let sit for about two or three weeks and then when the rats that are making burrows in the trash on the street hit about thirteen inches long nose to tail, they perform a mass eviction and bulldoze the entire mess of trash right into the compactor, rats and all.

When coming out of a drain pipe on Skid Row, rats in Los Angeles seem to gain a lot of speed and hurl themselves about two feet into the air upon exiting the drains. So not only do you have the indignity of being poor, but there are MONSTERS that lurk and sniff and silently watch from the shadows and trash bins and hide underneath cars and hold still when the light hits them but you can always see their eyes, those bright yellow reflectors that freeze at attention.

And those little fuckers fly up out of the drain pipes.

I shit you not.

CHAPTER FORTY TWO

Los Angeles was really beautiful from my spot. I was about a kilometer away from downtown right on the embankment that separates the 110/10 freeway that cuts through downtown but I had a high up angled view of the city. It was a forested area, one of the few in the city that was not only inaccessible to foot traffic, but also had enough foliage to comfortably hide out in if you were homeless and needed to be left alone to sleep. I could see the lights of all the buildings downtown and it was a hell of a lot better than being down in all the rat and shit infested streets of the Missions.

It was peaceful, and my sleeping bag kept me nice and warm. I had enough dope and I slept fearlessly, no one knowing where my little spot in the trees was. There was no helicopter at seven in the morning, no gospel music blaring in my ears, no gang members trying to collect tax for sleeping in their territory, no escalator steps grinding over my head, and no danger of getting towed away in the middle of the night. This was my home. I was thankful for it.

It was a little chilly at night, but being California, it never got below forty-five Fahrenheit. I was always comfortable in my sleeping bag and kept a few extra blankets close by just in case it got too cold. When it rained I had another spot close by just under the freeway overpass on the other side of the bridge I was near. It was just a gravel lot in between two streets, one going on the freeway and the other getting off, but it was dry. Some nights it would start to rain about three in the morning, and I had just enough shelter to keep me dry if it didn't rain too hard or for too long.

Sometimes I'd sleep through the rain and wake up to find my blanket soaked through. This made for a very uncomfortable night; even if it stopped raining I had no way to dry out my stuff and my other blankets would already be soaked. The first time this happened was the coldest night I ever spent in my life. My gear was soaked through and I tried to keep warm but there was no way around it. Luckily for some reason I had a candle I used for reading and I propped up a blanket with a stick to make a little lean-to, lit the candle and closed up the tent.

Within a few minutes the temperature inside the makeshift tent was nice and cozy. My feet were unavoidably soaked but I just made room for them as well. I didn't sleep the rest of the night, but I didn't freeze to death either. I made sure to buy a box of long burning candles next chance I got. They came in handy on more than one occasion.

CHAPTER FORTY THREE

I was now getting to be a regular on the morning crew. There were the same ten guys on the corner of 5th and Broadway every morning starting about five a.m., and we all got along and respected each other's hustle. We even helped each other out, guiding customers to the right guy when someone showed up looking for whatever. There was Joe the white guy heroin dealer for the gang, Major and Ron, two black guys who sold pills, Vicodin, OxyContin, Colonopin, etc., Rasta, the kind of crack dealer, Jose and Martin, two Latino dealers who worked for the gang, Kerry, a diabetic who hung around looking to hook people up with dope to try and make a few bucks before starting his day picking up bottles and cans, Tex, and old white drunk who always smelled like liquor and was missing all of his teeth, Emily, a beggar street urchin who was always getting arrested for shoplifting, and a wide assortment of other characters who floated in and out during the day.

The traffic flowed along with the dope, and that action was dictated by a number of variables. It was as complex and fluid as a free market could be, and how much money you made depended on the weather, where the cops were stationed that day, when the gang decided to let dope out on the street and how much, if the purple shirts were in the area and if they were being assholes, if the shopkeepers chased you away from the front of their stores, the list goes on and on. The higher ups from the 5th and Hill gang were getting used to me being there as well. At first they avoided me, not really knowing who I was but it doesn't take too much asking around to figure out I wasn't a cop.

Undercover cops were almost too easy to pick out. Everyone who worked the morning crew knew each other, so if someone was standing around looking out of place for too long, you knew they were an undercover cop. People who wanted dope wanted to get in and out of there as quickly as possible, so they didn't hang around. The cops also used street language they were almost certainly taught at the academy, and it was almost comical to hear them try it out sometimes. They were almost always too overweight to be heroin users, plus all they did to look like they were junkies was not shave for three days.

Junkies have a kind of radar that gay people seem to have also. You can always pick out your own kind. You know what subtle little hints in body language, dress, and demeanor that give it away. I don't know why they even bothered using undercover cops. Catching drug dealers down there was like shooting fish in a barrel. If you just parked in an unmarked car for a few minutes anywhere along Broadway between 5th and 6th within five minutes you'd see a deal go down. There were even cameras on my corner, one directly across the street that was pointed right at us, and another across the street the other way that was enclosed in a circular bubble so it could get a 360-degree view.

Every once in a while the news would do a story on drug dealing in the city on the six o'clock news, and they'd use footage from those cameras. People would be talking about it all the next day, "Did ya see me on the news? They got a close up of me, Mark, and Tre. We were slingin' to some college kids and they got us doing the deal and showed it on the news!!" I never heard about anyone getting busted from those surveillance cameras, or anyone in court having footage used against them.

The average time I noticed a dealer working the streets was six months to a year. They kept up as many dealers as they needed, and there was always someone to replace whoever got popped. I'd get to know all the new guys as they came along. I was starting to get a good reputation for guiding buyers to dealers, so the dealers were always coming up to me to ask me to bring them customers. Once in a while, one of them would throw me a bag of dope for bringing them a good sale, so those were the guys I brought customers to. I had a cell phone as well, so if a dealer had to make a call, needed a phone and kicked me down, he was sure to up his business twenty to fifty percent by being on my good side.

I was getting to know all of the buyers who were down there EVERY day, and I knew who the good dealers were, so I was starting to hook a lot of people up. I usually made about five or six extra bags a day, so along with the thirty to sixty dollars I made selling needles, I could stay well, eat good food, get new clothes, and keep clean. I thought it was important not to look like a street junkie. I was only selling needles and didn't feel like I was in danger but wearing nicer clothes can make you invisible when the police are cruising the area.

I noticed how people reacted to me when I didn't get to shower or wash my clothes for a few days, so I bought some new sneakers, picked out a few changes of clothes, and kept myself respectable looking. I always wore black, because blood stains would get all over any other color. Sometimes you have to shoot up in a hurry, and you don't have time to clean up the blood that spills out of your arms, so it gets all over the place. I picked out a few nice collared black dress shirts, hooded sweaters, and black stretch jeans that allowed me to stash a bunch of dope in the crotch, and I was ready to go.

CHAPTER FORTY FOUR

The guy I got along with the best on the street was Joe. He was the White dealer for the gang, and I was more than happy to keep him well supplied with customers. Joe did not look like, nor was he, a gangster. In fact, he was the most non – threatening guy on the streets, and it was easy for people to trust him. He had a friendly smile, he didn't look like a dope dealer, and he was only about five feet two inches, making most other guys taller than he was and he was also a bit overweight and had a mustache, making him look like Nintendo's Mario.

I also let him use my phone to find the pack man, so we found it convenient to never stray too far from each other. He amazed me in that no matter how dope sick he was, he would hold out on his first hit until he made his first fifty dollars. He told me that he was always fronted his first pack of dope by the gang, so he had to make that money back and flip that three times before he was playing with his own money.

When you were fronted a pack, you had to pay back fifty dollars for it instead of the forty dollars it cost if you just paid for it up front. He could never get enough ahead to have forty dollars at the beginning of the day because whatever he had left over he wound up shooting that night. He put away more dope than anyone I had ever seen. If he had three packs of twelve balloons left over at the end of the day they would be gone by morning. He always threw me down a couple and even had an apartment on 6th and Beaudry not too far away from where I slept so I would come over at night and we'd shoot a bunch of dope and play video games.

Things like this were a rare treat. It made me miss life in the real world. Just sitting down to watch a football game with some friends or going on a date with some beautiful young girl I had just met seemed a million miles away from where I was at in my life, and I wondered if I would ever get to do those things again. Joe let me crash there for the night, so we talked about these things and got a good night's sleep. In the morning, he threw me a wake up hit which I wasn't expecting at all, so we spent a few extra hours relaxing and let other people supply the city with heroin and needles.

Joe had his routine down as well. He'd start the day at six or seven, get fronted his supply, and work until he paid it off, then take a half hour break to scoot home and fix. Sometimes I went with him so his customers had a way to get in touch with him, for which he slid me a balloon once in a while. He wasn't too selective about his customers and it worried me that sooner or later he'd serve the wrong guy and get robbed or busted. I was still crashing on the floor with my sleeping bag, but it was a lot better than sleeping out of doors. I had a key and could come and go as I pleased, plus with a dealer for a roommate I was fronted a bag of dope whenever I needed one. I always made sure to get him back.

Over the course of the first five years I lived in three different missions, my camping grounds outdoors, tent city, at least three or four different apartments with friends who needed rent money and another half dozen who didn't. Assorted girlfriends and music rehearsal studios also served as sleeping spots. This is why they called us transients. We were the nomads of the city, the modern day rolling stones. Wherever you stop for the night is your home, and the next day brought a whole new adventure.

Joe and I were working out as roommates better than any roommate I ever had. We were comparable in our neatness and temperament, so we were never fighting about stupid shit like normal roommates do. I even got to the point of fronting him the cash he needed in the morning to get his supply and got an extra bag in return. It worked out for him so that he got an extra bag out of it as well because he saved ten bucks not having to get it fronted, so it was a good operation. He had a PlayStation 2, so we got a few extra games and a second controller and dueled it out over Spider Man and Gran Turismo.

In such a cramped space, you had better find ways to share your time constructively, otherwise you'll be at each other's throats. We didn't get such good reception on television, there was only about an hour every night of tv so we'd watch the news. We were always asleep early, partly because we got up so early but mostly because the dope put us to sleep as soon as we got comfortable.

In an odd way, I was kind of happy for the first time in years. I had been in such a back slide for the last few years that I was terrified of what was going to happen when I hit bottom, but now that I was here, it didn't take me long to find my groove and get what I needed. The first year was hell, digging through trash cans and carrying those flyer bags at five in the morning, but I kind of think in a way that was paying my dues, and my name on the street was a trusted one. I knew if I kept working hard I would soon be able to find a way out of this mess, but at least I was on a slow uphill climb. Trying to have a life while still an addict is like trying to swim through mud.

Because Joe worked for the gang, he was expected to be the pack man every once in a while. He had never done it before, but it was a rule that all of the dealers had to take their turn carrying all of the dope for the day. It was a horrible risk because if you got caught with a hundred packs of dope, you were sure to get sentenced for at least three years. He asked if I wanted to help him, and I told him I would as long as I didn't ever hold the dope. He wanted me to take the cash and count it, and he'd throw the people the packs.

They promised him three hundred dollars for working from five thirty a.m. until three o'clock in the afternoon. I told him the stories about the other people I knew who were pack men that got ripped off, but he was obligated to do it, so I agreed to help. I also knew it would get me in tighter with the 5th and Hill gang, and that's always a good thing to do for protection- from them in particular, if no one else.

We got there on time, a parking garage on 7th street. The leader of the morning crew was there to meet us. He told us the rules, we'd get ten bags of ten packs of twelve balloons, collect forty dollars for each pack, and re up when we ran out. That was four thousand dollars we were supposed to turn in every time we re upped, so the money had to be counted from every dealer every time somebody picked up. That was my job. Joe wasn't good with money or adding, so I got to count the money that came in. I wanted to keep my reputation as a trustworthy person, and I wasn't a thief anyway, so they were okay with me counting the money.

We loaded up the backpack with as much dope as I had ever seen in my life and hit the street. The first rush was on. We were stationed about three blocks from where they sold the dope to the customers. We sold out of the first load we had within an hour and everything went smoothly. As soon as we loaded up the next pack, Joe asked me to go and load up a needle for him at the apartment. It was only ten minutes walking distance away, and he gave me a whole pack to load us up. I took off, loaded about four hits in a syringe for myself, and the same for him. I hit mine, damn near passed out and sat on the bed with my head between my legs drooping down to the floor. Luckily, I snapped out of it, and took Joe his hit. He grabbed it and threw me the backpack full of dope, and even though I didn't want to take it I didn't have much of a choice so I started taking calls and handing out dope to the dealers.

CHAPTER FORTY FIVE

You have to be flexible and prepared for the worst on the street, and the next series of events were as unexpected as could be but I had myself covered and came out unscathed, yet I was homeless once again. Joe and I got up early one morning to get to work, and he asked if he could borrow my phone to keep in touch with the pack man. I usually said no, I needed my phone and didn't want to take a chance of it getting lost, but he threw in a few bags to sweeten the deal, so I let him use it for the day. I slept in a few hours and got on my way to work. When I hit the streets, Joe was nowhere to be found.

I tried calling my phone, but there was no answer. Shit. I knew this was bad news and called every twenty minutes to try and find him. No one on the street had seen him. Some people had seen him earlier that day but not in the last few hours. I waited until night, went back to the apartment and he still had not arrived home. The next morning I called the rampart police station, and sure enough, he was in jail. I asked around on the street because someone had surely seen him get popped, and I found someone who had seen it happen.

When Joe hit the street the day before, he was the only dealer for some reason. He picked up a few packets and was immediately mobbed when he hit the street. There were a hundred people looking for dope, and he re-upped as fast as he could sell shit. Within an hour or so he had sold to an undercover. A patrol car zipped up, threw him in back, and took him away. I knew this was going to happen sooner or later, but I wish I hadn't given him my fucking phone. My phone was in jail with his property and there was no telling when I'd be able to get it back.

I figured he'd be gone for at least a month because he'd have a possession charge as well as a sales charge, and he could be gone anywhere from a month to several years. I asked a friend to move in, took half a month's rent from him, and wish I hadn't. He turned out to be a fucking thief, and I found a few things missing from the pad. I kicked him out immediately, and started looking for someone else to move in.

I went out to work as usual about a week after Joe had been arrested and came home to something I couldn't believe. The door to the apartment was taken off the hinges, and every single thing in the place was gone. The bed, the refrigerator, the television, all of the clothes, it was just empty. I couldn't believe it. I knocked on the landlord's door, he answered and told me Joe hadn't paid rent in three months, He told Joe he was getting kicked out a month ago. Joe had been taking my money and using it to buy dope.

Luckily, I told the landlord my story and he believed me, so he let me go through the stuf fhe took. I got all of my blankets, clothes, sleeping bag, and anything of Joe's I could pawn and split. I was living outdoors again, but I still had my spot, so I dropped off my shit, hit the pawn shop, collected sixty dollars, and picked up a pack for myself. I was still without a phone and figured I'd resolve that as soon as I got the cash. I couldn't believe within a few hours I had gone from having an apartment to being back out on the street again, but like I said, this was the kind of messed up shit that happens on Skid Row. I was really pissed off at Joe and made no attempt to get any of his things back.

The other strange thing that happened was I was approached by the 5th and Hill gang. Since Joe was in jail, they needed a new white guy to be on their crew. I met with the leader of the day shift and he explained the situation in a very business-like manner. It sounded like a good deal, but I was iffy about it. I would've loved to make the money and get free dope along with the street protection of the gang and the prestige that went along with it, but I didn't want to end up like Joe. Inevitably, that's where all dope dealers wind up.

They need new people on the crew constantly, and Joe was expendable, as I would be. I noticed they didn't make any effort to get him out of jail, and since I was still making good enough money with my own hustle, I respectfully declined the offer, thanking him for his confidence in me but I just wasn't the right guy for it. I made forty to sixty dollars a day selling needles, the cops didn't bother me, nor did anyone else. If I started slinging heroin, I was risking a lot.

About three weeks later, Joe was released from jail. I saw him on the street and ran up to him. He was sickly and underweight, and his skin was a strange color. I didn't ask him about it and it seemed he didn't want to talk about it, but whatever protection he got from 5th and Hill in jail was probably just enough to keep him alive, or at least in one piece. He asked me what the fuck happened at the apartment, and I told him the story. He actually had the nerve to be pissed off at me, saying he had been able to keep the landlord at bay for the last few months and I should've done the same. I was FURIOUS, telling him I had NO IDEA he hadn't EVEN BEEN PAYING RENT WITH THE MONEY I WAS GIVING HIM, AND IT WAS HIS OWN FUCKING FAULT.

We got into a fight in the middle of the street, and I told him to go and fuck himself. Even though we both continued to work the same corner, we both felt betrayed by the other and I never got my phone back. I never told him I pawned off half of his shit, but by that time the landlord had gotten rid of anything else. He didn't have the nerve to go back there and ask for his shit back, so he was out on the street as well.

I was back to living in my space above the freeway. It was still the last few months of winter, so I decided to move back indoors for a while and just use my place during the day. I went back to the Missions and signed up for a bed. It was nice getting breakfast every morning and sleeping in my own bed, but I missed having an apartment to call my own and it just gave me more incentive to try and get off the streets.

I decided to try and quit dope. I signed up for methadone from the clinic at Beverly and Alvarado.

CHAPTER FORTY SIX

The first problem I had was that there was a limited number of slots they had available to provide junkies with methadone. I was put on a waiting list, and in the mean time I was able to save up enough for a phone. New phones at Sprint cost several hundred dollars, but I was lucky enough to meet a guy on the street who was willing to sell his for forty bucks so he could get some dope.

Within a few weeks the clinic called me, and they said they had a space available if I wanted to start methadone treatment. The second problem was that they opened at five in the morning, and were only open until noon, and that was okay, but if you missed more than two days in a month, you were dropped from the program.

I still started the treatment with every intention of trying to quit. I was still making thirty or forty dollars a day selling needles, and I figured if this stuff worked I could keep away from dope because I wouldn't have cravings. Well, that was how it was SUPPOSED to work. Methadone was an opiate just like heroin, so you were still addicted to it. The difference was that methadone had properties that made it last all day, and you were supposed to lower your dose little by little and eventually get completely off of the stuff.

The program was for thirty days, and having gone through detox before, I was apprehensive about it. My last heroin kick took me six weeks to get well, so I was hoping the methadone would keep the sickness away. It might have worked, but I get distracted so easily that within a week I had already missed two days of treatment and was kicked off of the program. The few days I was dosing it kind of seemed to work, but there was no high like there was with heroin, just the absence of sickness, and a drowsiness that you could easily sleep the day away on.

There was another reason for me to keep my appointments at the clinic. Methadone comes in a thick red liquid which a nurse dilutes with a little water, and it tastes vile. It's a little like concentrated cough syrup with a bitter taste, so it's easier to chug it like a shot of Jack Daniel's. The nurse watches you take your dose, because people were holding their doses in their cheeks, spitting back into a cup and selling it on the street for twenty dollars. Methadone is just as in demand on the street as dope or pills, mostly from junkies who are trying to quit but can't get on the program. I swallowed the dose with a nasty look on my face, and nearly coughed it up.

"Here, this might help."

I almost fell over and certainly couldn't speak for a second. She was a petite brunette with full red lips and shiny, black lustrous hair that girls in shampoo commercials have. She was wearing expensive designer clothes and had skin the color of tea with cream. I took the cup from her hand and sipped a little bit.

"Thanks. Do you work here?"

"No, I was in line before you and I think it tastes pretty nasty, too. I almost bust out laughing when I saw the look on your face."

"You're in the program? I mean, you don't look like you're an addict."

"Thanks, I'll take that as a complement. You don't look like you're an addict, either."

For once I was glad I made the extra effort to take care of myself. I usually wore clean clothes to avoid suspicion from the police. When you don't look like a street junkie you're less likely to get stopped and searched, but now it was paying off for another reason. I had forgotten about sex for so long I wasn't even looking for it, and the girls who hung around the places I lived were either too burned out or scandalous. I was used to dating Hollywood starlets and debutantes, models and college graduates, so the pickings on Skid Row were not the type of girls I was used to nor did I want to be.

"Thanks. Ummm, what's your name?"

"Fawn."

"Fawn?"

"Fawn."

Her name was Fawn. I loved that.

"Wait, well, umm, I guess I'll see you here, right? About what time do you come here?"

"You'll have to stick around and find out", she said with a sexy little smile that let me know she wanted me to find out. I was hooked. I hadn't even THOUGHT about a woman since I couldn't remember when. My days of Hollywood nightclubs and D.J. ing exclusive after hours parties were far back enough clouded in my memory by dope that the dream girls who haunted them and I had loved were a distant memory.

I watched her walk away in those velvet covered high heels, those black and white pumps that looked so great with those stockings and that hair, that hair that was thick and smelled great and looked incredible. If she were swimming in a pool of ketchup that hair was going to look great.

I was at the clinic early the next morning, showered, dressed, and pressed, and sat there for two and a half hours before she showed up again. I didn't want her to know I was waiting all morning for her, but I DID want her to know that I was hoping to run into her, so I brought a couple of sodas from the store. She showed up looking sweet as could be, wearing a dress that was slit up the side and grinning like it was Christmas morning. I held out one of the sodas for her and she took it gratefully. What a smile. Perfect teeth and white as snow. Fire engine Revlon Red lipstick. She was a bit dolled up today as well.

"Thanks. I try to remember to bring something with me but I always forget."

"Why don't you go get your dose and then we'll get something to eat? It'll be my treat."

"I've got a better idea. Let's stop at the store and pick up a few things, then we can go to my place and we'll cook something healthy. I can't stand fast food."

It was the best better idea I have ever heard in my life.

"God, I haven't been able to cook in a while. I'm really good at it. I can even make it vegetarian if you want."

"Sounds good. Wait for me here."

I was excited to see her but a bit apprehensive. I was in a bit of a quandary, because I preferred classy, intelligent women like she seemed to be, but what kind of classy intelligent girl dates heroin addicts? (ones with psychotic ex boyfriends naturally). I told myself this was self-defeating thinking and wanting to spend time with her regardless of that. I put those thoughts away and talked to some of the other addicts on the steps outside of the clinic until she came out.

"Are you ready? Let's go."

The other guys I had been talking to enviously watched me walk away. Most of them were homeless street guys and looked it. The people who had jobs and looked like they didn't belong here never stuck around, they just swallowed their dose and took off. The clinic was always one of the best places to score as well. It was a concentrated nest of addicts, and you could be pretty sure none of them were undercover cops, so finding dope was as easy as asking someone.

They all still had their connections regardless of the fact that they were using methadone, and probably about half of them were just on the program to get their morning hit for free. They'd be off and scoring as soon as they left the clinic so it wasn't uncommon to see three or four people get in a little huddle, talk about quality, price, and availability of their dealer's dope, and scramble off to go and score.

We decided on some pasta and a few cheeses along with some vegetables. I was starting to feel almost human again. It's the little everyday things that you miss, but you don't even really know you miss them until you come back to them. I was getting into my more serious mode, and we talked about movies that we liked, the last book we read, what we were reading now, and I was quickly falling for her.

We jumped on the subway and head over to her place. She was living in the Pegasus, a high-rise building on 7th and Flower, right in the middle of downtown. It was only about a ten-minute walk away from where my sleeping spot was. I was happy she was close but I decided to be honest with her about my situation and see how she reacted to it.

Her apartment was small, and the view was facing inside the square in the middle of the building, but I got the guided tour, and the rest of the place was spectacular. There was a gym, a sauna, and the roof deck was immense. There was a pool with thirty deck chairs for sunbathing, tables for picnics, and a computer room with about six workstations built into it. I spent a few minutes checking my email, sent a few replies, and we went back to her place to eat. I grabbed a quick shower, cooked up a tasty lunch, and we never stopped talking.

Apparently, she was supposed to be in school and hadn't told her parents she quit, so they were still paying the bills. She got a grant to go to college and spent the grant money on dope for herself and her now ex-boyfriend. He had been leeching off of her for the last six months and had never given anything in return. She was a nice girl, and I could see how someone could take advantage of her. I also did not discount the possibility that she wanted me around because she was afraid of this guy. It wouldn't be the first time a girl I dated was in fear of an ex- boyfriend. I couldn't blame a single one of them.

I thanked her for lunch, but I needed to make a few bucks before the day was out. Since she was so close by, I knew we could see each other whenever we wanted to. We exchanged phone numbers, and I grabbed a few needles at my spot. I couldn't stop thinking about her and something didn't make sense. It's one of those things you can't put your finger on, but you don't know what it is. You have to solve the riddle on your own, so I went to see the Oracle of Skid Row.

CHAPTER FORTY SEVEN

The Oracle of Skid Row was this little old lady who lived in the Cecil Hotel on 6th and Main street. She knew everything about everybody, and all she was missing was a crystal ball. She had gotten some kind of inheritance and every few months she would show me a check for ten grand she had received in the mail. Instead of moving back into the real world, she preferred to stay on Skid Row and smoke crack all day long.

Her name was Paige and she was in pretty bad shape. She was maybe four feet nine and so skinny her ribs showed through her back. Her body was wrecked from years of addiction and scars from infections and abscesses had taken their toll on her skin. She was wizened and old with grey scraggly hair and only a few teeth left in her mouth, but she had a genuine smile like Ruth Gordon in "Harold and Maude" and never seemed to be without visitors. She walked with a cane all bent over and shushed away attempts to help when she stood up or sat down, and never hesitated to order a pizza when I was there.

I think that she was afraid to be alone and not without good reason. The hotels and apartments of Skid Row were filled with criminal sex offenders, most of whom had a thirty day room after getting paroled. Once they found out there was a single woman living in the building, she was a target for the men. They knocked on their doors at three in the morning, they knocked on their doors at seven in the morning. If they saw the woman in the hallway, they would follow them to their room. The women would be terrorized as the men follow them at close range always with the intention of getting into their room with them and then it would be their word against the woman's.

It was a very dangerous world for the women of Skid Row. Paige would not be able to defend herself against a small terrier much less a full grown man, and I know she felt safer with me there. The fact that she bought a large amount of crack every day meant that the dealers knew she had the funds, and this also made her a target.

She and I had spent a lot of time together and she always was willing to put me up for the night if I was desperate. I supplied her with fresh needles, no charge, and whenever I stayed in her room she bought crack for both of us and never asked for anything in return. She sat in her room knitting hats of all colors she sold on consignment in stores on Melrose Avenue. I'm not even sure where she came from- it's as if she had always been on Skid Row, that's how she knew so much about everybody.

"Fawn, huh? Yeah, I know her. Her ex is a loser. He would yell at her to give him the biggest piece of dope when they scored together, even though she always paid. He was a real asshole. I think he's still around, stalking her. Did you sleep with her yet?"

"No, but I'd like to. I don't know, something doesn't seem right. I mean, everyone's got their skeletons in the closet, God knows I do, but she and I get along really well, and we're just friends for now."

"Be careful. She is a sweetheart, but she's got a lot of baggage she's carrying with her. She may need you more than you need her, and there's always a price to pay with girls like her. It may look like a good deal from your perspective, but as soon as you get involved, BAM! Whatever she's carrying around sneaks up and tries to eat you, and then it's your problem too."

 "So, you know what it is? "

"I know a few things that you don't, things she wouldn't want anyone to know. I can't tell you what they are, all I can say is watch your back, and know that if you do get involved you'll get more than you bargained for."

Everyone has a Yoda like person in their life, and Paige was mine. After that heavy conversation, we got some rock, smoked up and had a laugh. She couldn't walk very well, so I would always go and score for the both of us. She would buy my hit for going to get it, and I never took advantage of her generosity, nor she mine. She always seemed to know dealers who were close by and would sell anytime, day or night, yet she never seemed to really leave her little room. When she sent me to pick up, she always told the dealer I was her boyfriend when she called them so they would sell to me. That's what she told me, but I think she wanted people to think we were together. I let it slide because she really had a good heart and it was to keep her safe. We watched movies on cable for a few hours, and I crashed on the floor. In the morning I scored a few bags for us and went back to work.

CHAPTER FORTY EIGHT

The sound of a truck rolling by startles me out of my sleep. I sit up, confused, not knowing where I am for a minute. The sun isn't up yet, but it's light out. I was dreaming of my old life. Some people fantasize about the future, I have dreams about the past. I once d.j.'d for the WBCN river rave in Boston, and I was onstage with Blink 182 and The Red Hot Chili Peppers. I met a gorgeous Polish girl, and we made love in my room, a five star suite at some fancy Boston hotel, ate good food, and flew off to my next gig. This was my old life. Now I slept on the side of the freeway, sold needles to junkies on the street and hooked people up with heroin dealers for money.

I keep asking myself how I blew it, but I know the answer. Heroin. It all comes back to Heroin. It wasn't an overnight failure, it took years. I quit booking gigs, blew all of my cash, lost my studio, and finally hit bottom. I had no one to blame but myself, and here I sat, in a sleeping bag on the side of the freeway, selling needles to junkies. Was there any way out? Was I just going to get older and lose all of my teeth and become one of the invisible people on the street? Would the world forget about me and my music, my beautiful, beautiful music, and just let me die here, unknown and alone? Only time could tell, but it was a question I asked myself daily. I had to get to work.

I walked the ten blocks slowly to the intersection where I sold needles. I started out practically in the forest, my spot was so green with foliage and trees and I buried myself under the canopy of the branches and leaves. I walked over the bridge towards the city, passing the beautiful architecture and landscaping of the library.

I can see Pershing Square, the strange, towering sculptures painted purple and a fountain like a giant L with water pouring out of it. The air still smells good this time of day and passing the park I can see the first junkies of the day nodding off on the park benches, and I know it'll be my turn soon. I pass the red line subway station, the last stop on the way to work. The police sit there at the top of the steps looking for I don't know what, but they're there every day. I can see my corner now already in action, it has been since five thirty this morning. I'm one of the last ones here, and everyone tells me I could've made a lot of money if I were here earlier. There were a lot of people looking for needles, and I sell five right away.

I get my hit, my first of the day, and walk to Pershing Square. I know I could make a lot more if I hung around and served all the people who are walking around the block, but they can wait. I sit under the trees and unwrap my works, cotton ball, little tin metal cup I use to cook in, fresh needle, clean water, lighter, dope, rubber tie to raise my veins. I can smell the opium as the little brown ball of dirt dissolves in the water, one of the most pungent aromas you would ever smell, and I know the dope is good this morning. It changes from day to day, and if you can smell it from far away like today it's good.

It burns my fingers holding the tin cooker, so I set it aside and pull a needle out of a sterile wrapper, roll a little cotton ball, and throw it in the cooker. It pulls out dark brown, a muddy river, a warm gun, and I tie my arm tight. The veins rise just enough today. I slide the needle in and I hit on the first try. Red fountains spurt up in the syringe, it's a clean hit. I untie the rubber band around my arm, take the plunger and push it in slowly. Too fast and it might come out, slowly, and it all goes in painlessly.

First I taste it in the back of my throat. It'll only be three seconds now and the cloud comes over my head, the feel of bees walking on my face, a thousand of them, the warm rush of morphine on the brain, the twenty-thousand-year-old rush, passed down from generation to generation, eaten, smoked, drank, shot. We concentrate it and shoot it. The dope is good this morning. I think I'll get a doughnut, one of those wonderful doughnuts, maybe a chocolate milk & & maybe & & & & ....

I wake up and the sun is over the towers. I pick up my head from between my knees and put my needles away, wondering how much money I could've made if I had just stayed and worked instead of nodding of f in the park. It doesn't matter, some days are good, some days are slow, but sooner or later, I wind up in the park, head between my knees, asleep.

I slowly walked the block while I ate, bringing myself back to life and assessing the situation. Who was working, who was looking, who was guarding, if there are any undercovers, all normal things I look for. The leader of the day crew, a tall Mexican named Paulo was at the far end of the block. I had rarely spoken to him, except to verify someone's credibility or exchange information about informants and undercovers.

He wore expensive athletic jackets and new Nike's and always had at least two soldiers with him. He never carried anything but he was in charge of who worked, who carried, and who was the pack man for the day. Whenever he passed by me, he wouldn't even acknowledge me except for a slight nod once in a while, nor I him unless there was something to discuss.

Paulo sent one of his soldiers my way. I didn't think it had anything to do with me, so I turned my head and went about my own business. His name was Rassa, I knew him as being one of the enforcers. He was a tough character, shaved head with skull tattoos, ink all up and down his arms, baggy Dickies and a gold tooth. I gave the higher ups and enforcers free rigs. They never asked for more than they needed, nor did they take advantage of me, but I figured it was better to be on their good side. I thought he was going to ask me for some points, so I reached in my bag for a few.

"Hey, Blanco, Paulo wants to see you."

I wondered what he wanted to see me for. Usually it was to ask if I had seen something or someone, since I was on the corner a few hours a day I was an extra pair of eyes for them, and reporting to the gang on what happened here or there was not uncommon. I put the rest of my doughnut away and stashed my milk in my bag as I walked up. Paulo reached out to shake my hand, and I took it knowing this was going to be more than a few words.

"How you doing, it's Ivan, right?"

"Yeah, doing good, you know, making money, What's up?"

"I got a little proposition for you. What would you think about working for me?"

"What do you got in mind?"

"You know everybody, everybody knows you. You know who the buyers are. You been hooking up a lot of my guys with customers. I need a solid person to handle about twenty regulars and still work the street. You only go with people you know, you don't have to take on any new business unless you want to so you won't take a chance on selling to no undercovers. But I need a white guy on the day team, and everyone says you're okay. I think you're okay. You get protection day and night, and if anyone fucks with you, you come to us. We can front anything you need, as long as you get it back, so you'll never be hurting. You use?"

"Yeah I use."

"So do most of the guys on the street crew. That's okay, it comes out of your own pocket, but don't get caught with a dirty needle or cottons. Leave that shit somewhere else. You can make a lot of money, as much as you want depending on how much you use, but you can't lose. Just stick with the people you know, and you'll never sell to an undercover. So, are you in?"

"What about Joe? I thought he was the white guy on your crew.

He laughed a little bit, a very condescending laugh that let me know that he had no respect for Joe.

"Man, that little fools crazy. He shoots more than he sells, and he's missing half the day. I need someone to be around all morning, and you can still sell rigs as a cover."

"Lemme think about it okay? I appreciate the offer, but I got a few other things going right now. Lemme see what's going through and what's not, and I'll talk to you in the next few days."

He had a look on his face like Are you crazy? EVERYONE on the street was dying for the chance he had just offered me. Free dope, protection, MONEY, was I fucking INSANE? Inside I was excited- they had asked me to work for them before, and he knew I had turned them down. In reality I was just a face for them, someone to get busted if undercovers walked in. But he was right, I DID know everyone, all of the buyers, all of the sellers, and I wouldn't have to take any chances.

I shook his hand and walked away, excited at the whole ordeal. He was right about Joe. Joe was about as flakey as a person could get. He had no business being a dope dealer and sooner or later he was going to fuck up. He already HAD fucked up as far as I was concerned, but if he fucked over the gang, he was going to wind up dead. I had a few bucks saved up, so I took the rest of the day off to think about Paulo's proposal.

I knew what it meant. It meant someone to answer to. I wasn't very good at that. I was used to being my own boss. I was in charge. Now someone else would be in charge of me, but it was someone that knew if I was in good shape, he would make more money. He wasn't your typical thug. He was more like a capo, running an organized criminal unit with precision and dexterity. That took more than nerve, it took brains. And the fact was that out of all of the thousands of junkies and hustlers on Skid Row who wanted this position, he chose me.

CHAPTER FORTY NINE

I knew what the consequences were as well. Three years for trafficking. If it was just possession I might get off with Prop 36, a program designed to keep the jail population to a minimum. Prop 36 was a bill that kept possession of a minor amount still a felony, but without jail time. You had to report to drug diversion classes once a week and pay $30 each time you went. At the end of six months, if you got an okay from the drug diversion counselor the charge was taken off of your record. You could get this quite a few times before getting hit with a sentence that forced you to do time.

I decided to try it for a week or two and see how it fit me. I showed up early the next morning around five thirty and no one was there yet. I sold a few needles and talked to the addicts who were waiting for someone to show up and got some coffee. After about a half an hour a black SUV pulled over on the other side of the block and a few guys jumped out. Everyone knew better than to rush them. They were here to serve the individual dealers packs, and they would serve the junkies. Paulo was with them, so I waited a few minutes until the initial rush of customers was over.

I walked over to him, his guards checking me like I was some kind of a cop and motioned to him I wanted to speak to him in private.

"Okay, I'll try it for a week, but if for any reason it doesn't work for me, I get to go back to selling rigs. No territory dispute, no tax, it just goes back to the way it was, ok?"

"Why, what do you think is going to happen? "

"Nothing in particular I can think of, but right now I don't have to worry about getting arrested- the cops don't care about needles, and since I can swallow any shit I buy if I keep it in my mouth, I don't have to worry about getting charged with possession. If I work for you, I have to keep a few packs stashed on me somewhere, so I gotta worry about it. Plus, they might do a sweep of this place, I've seen them do it before, so if I back off, I'll let you know why but if my radar says danger, then I'm out. If that's cool with you, then let's do it."

"Yeah, that's cool. Joe's off duty for a while. He might bitch to you and ask why you're taking his spot, but it's MY word. What I say goes, so just tell Joe to come and talk to ME, okay?"

 "Okay. Any more rules?"

"You can start every morning between six and nine, but no later than ten. You can only work until three o clock, that's when the second shift comes on and if you sell on the street, I can't answer for you, so have anyone call you after three. Look out for the other dealers, and they'll look out for you.

You'll have your own clients after a week or two, so don't worry about who gets which buyer, they'll come to you soon enough. Some white guys don't trust us, so they'll only go through you. They think for some reason your bags are bigger, or you've got better dope, even though it all comes from the same place. Let them think that, it only insures they'll keep coming back to you."

"If you have any trouble, especially with the other dealers, come to ME. Some guys might try to tax you. Don't let them intimidate you, they're not supposed to. They might come and say that you're supposed to give them one of your packs and I said so but call me first. There's a lot of guys on the crew who don't want a white guy with us, but it's good for business so if they give you a hard time, let me know, let it slide, and think about the money you're gonna make."

"Packs are forty bucks each, fifty if you need the first one fronted, but don't go shoot up in some bathroom and then fall asleep and not make us any money. Don't be short. If you are, you might get away with it once, maybe twice, but if you're found out, you'll never work for us again. You call the pack man or call me to find out where he is. Get your money straight BEFORE you get to him, slide it to him and he'll give you the stuff.

We don't count cash in the middle of the street, but he'll put each guy's money in a different pocket. When he gets in the car he counts it all out, and you better be square with yours. You get one fuck up, second one, you're out. Joe said you fronted him the money a few times to get his stuff in the morning, so I assume you're better with money than he was."

"Don't talk to me or any of the other higher ups. We'll talk to you at the end of the day at the lot where we meet. No one can see us there, no one has anything on them so even if I'm standing right next to you, call me on the phone and talk to me that way. I'll let everyone know you're working for ME now, so if anyone says anything to you about selling on this block, you tell them to talk to me. I haven't told anyone yet, I didn't know what your answer was gonna be, so not everyone's gonna know right away. Anything you want to ask me?

I wanted to ask about getting bailed out of jail if I got caught. I know they've done that for the bigger dealers and higher ups, but it was much too soon to ask about such a thing. I'd wait until I was making them some good money, show them I was worth it, then ask them.

"Yeah, what are the boundaries? I can't just walk up and down Broadway all day."

"You can go anywhere from the freeway (six blocks west) to Los Angeles (three blocks east). Outside of that, you're in other people's territory, so you can meet people there but don't be selling on the streets near McArthur Park, that's MS-13 territory, they'll cut you into pieces. Past Ninth street is 18th street gang territory, and they'll jump you if they know you've got money or dope on you, so don't even go there."

"Oh yeah, and once you've established yourself, don't go down past San Pedro without one of us. Once all the blacks know you're working for us, if you go that way you'll get jumped for sure. They'll figure you've either got money or dope on you, so only go there if you've got business, and in that case take someone with you. Call me and I'll get someone to go with you. You got to kick them down but you won't get jumped."

"Make sure you count the money before giving someone the dope. EVERYONE will try to rip you off or shortchange you, so always tell them money first. If they say no, then they don't have the full amount. That's how you know. You've been here long enough so that the people you sell to will know you're good to your word anyway, so they won't try anything. Stick with the people you know. Everyone is going to want to buy from you but pick your customers. Don't let them pick you."

He took me over to the pack man, introduced me, and I picked up my first pack of dope. Paulo shook my hand, introduced me to a few others and told me he would point me out to the rest of them. I walked away slowly, as if I had been doing this all of my life. I put six balloons in my mouth and the rest under my balls. Within five minutes I saw someone I knew.

"Hey, I need two points. Who's working today?"

"I am."

"You're working now? Thank God, I need your phone number. You got six?"

"Yeah"

I took him around the corner and spit out six balloons. Thinking quickly, I asked for thirty bucks, which he already had in his hand. I gave him my number, and he said he'd be here at the same time every day for six. I sold the rest in the next five minutes, almost the same circumstances. Within ten minutes I had my first two regulars. I started thinking about how much money I could make. It took me about three hours to make twenty dollars selling needles, more if it was a slow day.

I had just done the same thing in five minutes.

CHAPTER FIFTY

They say some people are survivors. I used to think that meant you didn't die. Sometimes life can be worse than death. That's the life of a Skid Row junkie. They're beggars, thieves, con artists, hookers, they turn tricks, sell fake dope, look for scared white kids to rip off, they strongarm old ladies and men, they go into people's tents when they're asleep and get impaled with nails in a board. They get shot. They get raped. They go insane from the constant racket around them and start baying at the moon. They are outside suffering. They are cold, they are hungry, they get wet when it rains.

I knew what being a survivor meant. I never lost my dignity. I never had to do anything I would look back on and feel ashamed about. Anyone who I sold dope to was already an addict. We had no choice.

Everyone wanted to be my friend. Everyone was glad I was now on the crew. The first few days were rough but only because there were some members of the gang who either didn't know I was working for Paulo or didn't want me on the crew because they knew a lot of business would be turned my way. I had Paulo behind me, I was good to my word, so I had a lot more people on my side than not.

I learned quickly that I had to be tight with everyone, and I always took the money first. Everyone thought they were going to get a deal from me, or rip me off, but no one got the better of me. Every sale I made, I walked the customer off the block, out of the way of the cameras and cops, and counted the money. Everyone was short. I didn't let it slide, not even a dollar. I wouldn't take change either, and about a third of the people who came to buy from me had some of it in nickels and dimes. I told them come back when it was all in bills.

Everyone bitched and whined, everyone had a story about why I should cut them a deal, everyone tried to rip me off, but I ALWAYS counted the money first. After two weeks, everyone knew to have their money straight or I wouldn't sell to them and it went a little more smoothly. And with that, the money started to come in.

The first thing I did was to get some new clothes. Not nice clothes, I wanted to be invisible. I used to wear jeans, fatigues, boots, black shirts, flight jacket. Now I had to blend in. If a cop looked down the street, I wanted to look like every other person on the block. I picked up some new custom sneakers, a hooded sweatshirt with "Los Angeles" across the front in old English lettering, and black ultra-baggy drop crotch short jeans. I also grabbed a few Dodgers hats, a chain wallet, a few pairs of large sunglasses, tall, nearly knee high white socks, and tight underwear. Tight underwear was the key to my success, and if all the dope dealers in the world listen to me, there will be 20% less drug busts nationally.

I kept my dope under my balls. Most guys kept it in their mouths, but I already knew how hard it was to swallow more than three and most guys are carrying two packs. Most cops will go through your pockets, look in your socks, your bags, in your mouth, under your cap, but they won't want to see your balls and ass unless you're behind closed doors. They need a reason to arrest you so it's rare they go that far. It's also illegal to strip search someone in the middle of the street, so it makes sense to keep it in a place where they can't find it. This way they can't bust you unless you sell to an undercover.. I left my needles, cookers, anything else incriminating close by, but I never carried them while I was working

My underwear saved me almost immediately. It was only my second week, and I was still learning the ropes when I picked up three packs from the pack man. There was an undercover car on the block and they saw the deal go down. I didn't see the car cruising along side of us as we walked away, but it sure as hell screeched to a halt in front of us at a red light. Three cops jumped out and grabbed the pack man, tearing through his bags and finding twenty packs of dope immediately.

My heart was thumping so loud I could hear it and I was praying to God for the light to change so I could walk on. I was pretending not to notice the pack man getting busted right next to me other than a curious glance. I prayed so fucking hard they didn't see me buy from him and he was just getting popped by an undercover who had pegged him earlier.

Finally the light turned green and as I stepped off the curb, I felt a hand on my shoulder. The guy pulled me back on the curb and handcuffed me. I dropped all hope. I was going to jail. I had two packs before I bought the three, so I had five packs stashed under my balls. I knew they saw me make the buy. There was no hope.

"Where's the dope?"

The officer was going in and out of my pockets, feeling my shoulders, my neck, everywhere.

"WHERE'S THE FUCKING DOPE?"

They already had the pack man in the car, along with a girl who had been carrying for him.

"I don't have any."

"BULLSHIT IF YOU FUCKING LIE TO ME I'LL MAKE YOUR LIFE HELL NOW WHERE'S THE FUCKING DOPE!?!"

"I just got a pack of cigarettes from that guy. They're in my side pocket. You can go through them if you want to. But I don't have any dope. Maybe that's what you saw."

He was FURIOUS, pulling up my socks, going in and out of my pockets for a THIRD time. He turned to his partner and asked, "Did YOU see him buy it?"

"Yeah, I saw him, why can't you find it?"

"LISTEN DON'T FUCK WITH ME. WHERE'S THE FUCKING DOPE?!?!"

"I don't have any. I didn't buy any dope"

I remembered what a lawyer once told me. There's only one thing to say to cops in this situation.

"Am I being detained, or am I free to go?"

The cop was pissed. He never stopped searching me. He went through my pockets over and over again, then looked at his partner, dumbfounded. He knew I was never going to incriminate myself now. Once you say that to a cop, you can fight it in court. That's ALL you should ever say to a cop. Don't make it easier for them to arrest you. He turned to his partner and shrugged his shoulders.

"What do you wanna do?"

A crowd had gathered to watch. I mean they had the sirens going and the cars pulled in sideways blocking half of 5th street. I could see at least six or seven people I knew, people I sold to, people I wouldn't cut a deal to. They would have loved to see me get busted. Some were my friends and were concerned but knew better than to get involved. I could hear the cops talking behind me and I was still frozen with fear but I held fast. They grabbed my wrists, and grudgingly took off the handcuffs.

"If I EVER see you buying dope around here I'll take you in, you got it?"

"Yeah."

"Get the fuck out of here."

I picked up my bag and FLEW up the street. It was three o' clock, my shift was done anyway so I sped up to my spot and pulled out my stash. I cooked up an extra large hit, breathed a HUGE sigh of relief, and got high. Thank you, tight underwear. It was a law I never broke with myself. I bought ten extra pair the next day.

CHAPTER FIFTY ONE

I had another good person on my side. His name was Carlos, and people called him C for short. He was kind of a foreman, keeping the day crew organized and running smoothly, but he was also a dealer. He was a bit sharper than your average person and worked with his cell phone tied to his ear. He was either putting out other people's fires, hooking up sales, or keeping the pack man supplied and in line. He had always gotten needles from me in the past, and I never had charged him for them, so we were already on good terms. He was actually glad I was on the crew. He told me if anyone messes with me, tell them I worked for him, or just call him and he'll straighten it out. I seemed to hear that from a lot of guys lately.

I learned a lot about gang life from him. Inadvertently, I was learning a lot on my own as well. A gang has to be well organized and disciplined, otherwise they fight over everything and tear themselves apart. For the most part, they organize to make money. The guys who ran the street dealers were smart, as smart as anyone I've ever met. They read books, knew about politics, dressed sharp, and kept away from the product.

The guys at the bottom were the most visible and abundant. They were the ones who had to prove themselves through war, whether interpersonal or in groups. They weren't as smart or resilient, so they had to make themselves useful through legwork. If they were on point, their girlfriends, wives, and children would be taken care of while they were in jail. If they were loyal, their rent was paid, their phone was kept on, and their kids were picked up from school.

I think that's the thing most people could never understand about gangs and how desperate people are to stay off of the streets. Most of them are living in poverty and never seem to have enough, so they must be innovative to keep their children fed and housed and that's where a lot of the purpose of the gang comes in. If you are a member and arrested, hospitalized, or otherwise unable to provide for your family, there are others who will try to take up the slack for you. If you are worth your weight, others will be making sure your family has everything taken care of.

Some people think gangs are all about violence and drugs, and that is certainly a very visible part of it. It is the part that they show most often on the news, ensuring that people see themselves as criminals and police as enforcers and enemies. This puts certain demographics at a significant disadvantage, wouldn't you agree?

Most of the guys in the gang were married, or at least had children from a girlfriend. The girls were always around and helping wherever they could. Most of them were sweethearts and once I got to know a few of them they'd bring me coffee in the morning, show me pictures of their kids, walk with me down the street to make it look like we were out shopping for the day, and laugh at my poor Spanish. That always made me feel good. If a guy trusts you with his woman, he trusts you. I took no advantage of that.

Whenever I went to someone's house to celebrate a good day of making money or just to get out of the ghetto, it was truly mi casa, su casa and I was expected to eat the most and flirt with the single women. I loved Mexican families. They always made you feel at home and wished for nothing but your comfort and loyalty, and they got it from me.

I knew I would never be asked to be a gang member nor did I ever have the desire to be one, but that didn't stop most of the junkies in L.A. from asking me, "How I get on with them? Tell 'em I wanna work and I'm for real. Tell 'em now, go on, call 'em and tell 'em I can sell more dope than they ever seen I got guys waiting on blah blah blah blah.." I had to hear it from everyone.

You think of gangs in terms of low income residents who live on the same block protecting each other and their territory. This wasn't like that. No one actually LIVED on 5th and Hill. In fact, most of them lived far away in the suburbs where they had houses. This was their sales territory and they protected it as if they DID live here. They were scattered all over the county, some as close as McArthur Park a few blocks away, and some drove here or bussed in from nearby cities like Montebello or Santa Ana.

It was a well-organized unit, kept close by cell phones, working orders, and a hierarchy that was similar to the Mafia. You didn't HAVE to show up for work every day, but if you didn't, you don't get paid. I often saw the leaders there at five thirty in the morning calling around to see who was showing up as enforcers, salesmen, and who would be the pack man for the day.

"Hey, who's working?"

It was Fawn.

CHAPTER FIFTY TWO

She was up early, dressed to kill and grinning from ear to ear. She had on a black navy pea coat with a leopard skin collar and these high heels and her black hair was all blowing in her face and she looked like a movie star. I hadn't seen her since I started selling dope, I had just been too busy. I hadn't forgotten about her but I knew she was on the methadone program so I didn't think she'd be looking for dope.

"Yeah, I am."

"Really? You're working now? Good, I need your phone number again. What are you doing right now?"

"I gotta work for a while, but I can take a break."

"Good, let's go to my place. You got points?"

"Yeah. I mean I can go get them." I was tripping over my own tongue and couldn't stop staring at her.

"Good, I need a few. Are you hungry?"

"Yeah, I haven't had breakfast yet."

"Okay, we'll go to my place, hit up, and I'll make you something to eat."

She was no longer a girl I had a crush on. She was the one thing left tying me to civilization. She was the frail and hopelessly irreparable line that wouldn't let me go down any further, and there really wasn't much left of me, but she clung to that last little bit like she really wanted it to be real, like I could pick myself up enough and make a life for us, a real life, people around us to love us, people to take care of each other, a family. Some people got families, and some families got people, and sometimes those people aren't good people and we fly away from those places and we all wind up somewhere else.

Many of us wind up here.

How I envy the children who were spoiled by their parents to the point that they always get what they want from other people by throwing temper tantrums and yelling and generally making everyone's life so miserable they eventually just give in to placate a grown person screaming. How wonderful life would be without the emotional scars and childhood traumas that make us need heroin and other drugs in the first place.

When I walk down the streets of Skid Row today, I see guys showing off bags the size of baseballs filled with crystal methamphetamine. It seems as if they get fronted as much of it as they want.

I'm not sure where it comes from, but for five dollars you can be laced all night and you can usually find someone to kick you down for free. I'm not joking; there are metric tons of that crap down here and it is making everyone even more crazy.

This is no accident.

CHAPTER FIFTY THREE

We talked as we walked to her high-rise apartment. She told me that the methadone was working okay but she just wanted to get high today. She knew I wasn't a pusher. If someone I knew was trying to quit, I wished them all the best, but if they came back to me asking for dope, it was their decision. I wasn't anyone's mom or dad, besides, trying to say no to a dope fiend who is hurting ....

Only opiate addicts know how bad the pain of withdrawal is and they are way more willing to give something to a person who can't make it through their detox because they know that when you decide to quit, you'll quit, and you'll drive twenty hours to get high if that's how far away the dope is and you've decided you aren't going to make it through withdrawal.

If I didn't sell to them someone else would make the money, so I served anyone whom I was familiar with. I stayed tight with my clients. There were enough junkies I knew that I didn't have to serve anyone I didn't know.

We hit up in the safety of her apartment and sat down to eat. I told her the story of how they had asked me to work for them, and the things that had happened since then. She told me about how her ex was still stalking her, and how she was still lying to her parents about going to school. She was really pretty. I was flirting with her, and I think she was enjoying it. We made plans to get back together later in the week, and she reminded me if I needed a place to crash I could come and stay. I asked if she was doing anything for the rest of the day and she said no.

I stayed until late the next morning. We had an ultra slow, romantic, heavy buildup lovemaking session on the bed while listening to some field recordings of tribes in New Guinea or Madagascar. It was a much needed burst of affection that I was wondering if I would ever feel with anyone again. I think she probably picked up on that. Women are natural healers and some are just very gifted at knowing what would pull you out of whatever funk you're in. Fawn was doing that for me. I would even consider getting clean for her, but I was in too deep with selling and it was going to end badly. I didn't want to put her through what I was about to face some time in the next six months or so. I was out the door and on the street at nine thirty.

Since I was in the business district, I had people meet me uptown. There was less of a chance of getting caught when you weren't right on Broadway because cops weren't looking for dealers and junkies up on Hope Street. It was crowded with business people on lunch break, Fed Ex vans making deliveries, shoppers visiting the jewelry stores and restaurants, and kids walking to and from the library.

It was easy to hide among them, so I met as many people as I could in this part of town. It was four or five blocks away from the pack man, so it took a little longer to re up, but that extra ten minutes I spent walking between different parts of town made the difference between feeling safe and feeling paranoid. When you were on Broadway, everyone knew why you were there. White guys walking by themselves were always looking for dope, so all a cop had to do was follow him until he connected then bust the dealer AND the buyer.

The problem with being a dealer was that I was shooting a lot more. I'd come home at the end of my shift, stopping on the way to get dinner. I'd get myself situated in my little thicket amongst the trees on the side of the freeway, eat what I brought, make a few phone calls, and shoot four or five balloons at once. I used to do them one at a time, but with a larger supply comes a larger habit, and I was able to do as much as I wanted. I usually had three of four packs with me by the end of the day.

I still took phone calls and had people meet me by my spot but for the most part I just shot myself into oblivion. I wrapped myself up in my sleeping bag, maybe read a book until the sun went down, and was fast asleep by seven thirty. I would sleep straight through until five thirty or six a.m.. If I ever woke up in the middle of the night and couldn't get back to sleep, I'd just slam three more balloons.

Waking up was the hard part. It was before sunrise, still cold and dark, and even though I'd had ten hours of rest the heroin made me groggy. When I had just one to go to bed with I'd wake up already dope sick. When I shot four before sleep and did three in the middle of the night, my eyes would be glued shut for half an hour while I tried to revive myself. I'd wake myself up with a shot, usually having difficulty finding a vein. All of my veins would be constricted from low circulation, so I had to stab myself several times before I got the needle to register a hit. By several times I mean up to a hundred one after the other, trying to draw up blood to show I hit a vein. On rare occasions it could take an hour or more.

My face would be streaked with spit and tears as I tried to soak all of the blood out of the needle through a cotton ball. This kept the needle from clogging as the blood from the subcutaneous level would coagulate in the syringe and clog up the needle. The most painful thing to happen is to finally register a hit (see blood flow back into the syringe, showing that you hit a vein) after an hour of trying, then upon pushing the dope in feeling the plunger stop because the needle was clogged. You could fight with it and draw back and blood will still come in the syringe but it will refuse to let the heroin past whatever is clogging it up, and you will have to start again.

It was a dream come true having dope every morning when I woke up. It usually took me around an hour from the time I woke up to the time I got my first hit in me when I was selling needles. Before that I wouldn't get one until early afternoon, so being able to shoot up before I hit the street enabled me to work until noon without taking a break.

CHAPTER FIFTY FOUR

My list of customers was growing fast and my phone was ringing all day. Half of my job was fighting with people over money. They'd call me up crying, telling me how their mother/ kid/ dog just died and they were totally out of cash and they needed a favor. I told them all the same thing. I told them I got people asking me for favors all day long, and I couldn't help everyone out. Funny, somehow within ten or twenty minutes they all found twenty bucks and still came to see me.

I never felt guilty about being a dealer. I wouldn't sell to anyone who wasn't already an addict. From selling needles for the last year, I knew who was hooked. I had kids come up to me and ask to buy, but I walked. You had to be no doubt about it addicted to buy from me. People who were curious about heroin or just got it once in a while to come down from a coke binge bought from someone else. This insured a daily clientele, plus safety from taking on an undercover as a customer. Believe me, there were PLENTY of junkies to keep us all busy all day. All I did was make it a little safer for them to buy.

The other thing I was finding out was that the more money you made, the more you spent. I thought I would be loaded with cash by the end of the first week. Instead, I was paying my storage space bill, my phone bill, buying clothes, eating at restaurants instead of at the missions and shooting a lot more dope. I sent my brother twenty dollars a day to save for me and took a lot better care of myself.

I was starting to figure that the only way I was going to get off the street was to start using a lot less dope. My habit had increased from twenty dollars a day to almost a hundred. Of course I got it wholesale so it only actually cost me about sixty dollars, but having as much dope as you wanted to shoot wasn't a blessing, it was a curse.

The other thing was that as my status rose and my pockets filled, I was aware I was being targeted. Muggings were common on Skid Row and if you didn't take precautions you got hit. My sleeping spot was west of the main strip, but the worst sections of Skid Row were east. I rarely had business in tent city or near the missions, so I avoided them. I especially steered clear once I was known as a dealer. Everyone would know I had either cash or dope on me, and not a small amount.

I called Fawn and asked if I could stop by.

She was just getting up. I think she had been smoking crack all night from the looks of it, that and the fact that she pulled out a pipe and offered me a hit. I rarely smoked crack but I thought it would be okay just once with her. I was starting to unwind a little bit. I told her about my day, and she seemed genuinely concerned about me and glad I was okay. I offered to take her out for dinner but she said she just wanted to chill indoors and watch movies on cable.

We ordered a pizza, and I took a shower. She had some sweats for me to change into so I dried off and put them on. We fell into bed, and she lay her head on my chest as I put my arm around her. We did it at the same time, and it felt natural and quite relaxing. Our breathing slowly synchronized, and we fell asleep snuggled in a ball.

CHAPTER FIFTY FIVE

The homeless is not a million people with one face. Each person has a gift, each person has a life they were good at something and for whatever reason lost it. Some find it again, some never do, but they are in constant need of help. If you give them money they will make the same poor decisions that led them to being homeless in the first place. If you give them jobs they will have to learn to be self sufficient or they will fall back down.

If you feed them you keep them under a security blanket that is so thin but must be kept going or they will riot, they will demand food and they will not stop until they are fed. This growing and eating and begging population of people who fell down and couldn't get back up, these people are our neighbors and parents and daughters and we went to school with them and went on first dates with them and wonder where they are now; these people are who lost and can't find their way out.

For so many, a simple form they can't fill out or even learning how to research on the internet how to stop from being foreclosed upon or evicted is too difficult of a concept to understand or pursue because there is no one for them to ask for help. There is no one who will give them the time to see if they are ok or if they are about to lose their social security benefits because they let it lapse or filled out the wrong form and they are afraid. They are on the streets and every day they are hoping to find a way out.

In some states in the U.S.A., a woman in need of finances can only legally perform a sex act for payment if they are shooting a pornographic movie. THIS is where the sex slavery comes in, because since prostitution is illegal in most states, whoever has a video camera can legally pay a girl for sex. THIS is where the problem really becomes apparent, and how pimps and gangsters are able to control the laws with just as must shrewdness as the best lobbyist on capitol hill.

Since the girls' only option for making fast and obviously much needed cash is to agree to be filmed, it has a dual advantage for predators who know how to work it. Since the girls only have one option, they don't get paid any more for fucking on film (since it's the only way to do this legally). The people who shoot the films can now make money of fof uploading it on the internet (not sure how that breaks down but I know porn $$$ goes into the billions). Predators can also use the film as blackmail, and when other methods fail, they stalk and threaten girls.

A lot of the women on Skid Row have been victims of sex slavery, but of a much different kind. They are regularly beaten and raped and will be sold for a pittance. Many of them stare at the ground in a state of perpetual shock. Others will talk loudly and endlessly about whatever comes to mind, and still others work as drug holders or lookouts. Whatever it is they do to deal with it, it is guaranteed there's someone with a stranglehold on her and is probably beating her. They must put up with the most degrading kinds of perversions and they can be extreme. Skid Row is home to the highest number of sex offenders in the world, I think some 15 percent of the population has at least one sexual offense, that's nine thousand convicted sex offenders in a ten-block radius.

I have heard them cry about abusive boyfriends, abusive fathers, brothers, even sons. I've hidden them in my apartment while pissed off thugs roam the hallways and kick the doors looking for the woman shaking and shivering in terror next to me. A gang member had been holding a woman hostage in her room and sexually assaulted her. He also threatened her to let him stay and now he was in our hallways at night calling out his gangster shit and making everyone miserable.

The police came time and time again and were never able to do anything to help her without her signing a complaint, so he stayed and beat her up in the hallways and acted a fool every night. Finally, we had enough and moved her into another room and sealed the one she had been in up to make it look like she moved away.

This was the lowest person I had ever run into on Skid Row. He was probably twenty-three or so, tall and built, and she is perhaps sixty-one or two years old, and more than a bit overweight. She would run out of her room to mine and bang on the door to be let in, terrified he would see her. He would either be on the roof trying to break in her window or in the hallway kicking in her door.

The police came because another little old lady was terrified by the pounding and called 911. They handcuffed this guy, took down all of his information, but without a crime, they had to let him go and the old lady was too afraid to tell the police he didn't belong there and was terrorizing her into submission and sexually assaulting her every chance he got.

Since the little old lady was too afraid to come out and the police she called were downstairs banging on the door, I had to go downstairs and tell them everything was fine. Except everything wasn't fine; those motherfuckers saw me talking to the cops and thought I was the one who called them to complain. For that they executed my cat.

CHAPTER FIFTY SIX

Rarely is there a place for these women to go. Battered women's shelters do exist but they are communal living areas and are not very nice places to be at all. The showers in my building are constantly being disinfected and bleached from the previous night's activity, and used condoms are an unpleasant reminder that this place is diseased.

There was one girl who was brought over by Z. Z was Carl Zephyr, who had been playing bass on one of the tracks I was working on. He had been in Rick James band for 15 years, and the constant "I'm Rick James, BITCH!" stories were well worth the middle of the night interruptions, the drug pipes that came out and I had to extinguish, the strangers dumped on my front doorstep, and other middle of the night dramas that seemed to follow Z like Pigpen's cloud of ever present dust.

In all honesty he could probably still be one of the greatest bass players living today. He schooled me in funk and I taught him computers. He knew every player on every record from Motown to Casablanca and would yell out stories of bands he played in with that person, being on the road with them, or meeting them at a funk jam in some big city, and he had stories about everyone.

Z showed up one night with a girl he was raving about that could sing, as we had been looking for a singer. I was immediately struck by her appearance. She had the sunken cheeks and sadness of an addict and kept a head scarf wrapped around her face. Her clothes were brown rags, dirty from the street and she was in her filthy socks, no shoes. I could tell this girl had just been through so much sadness and pain I didn't have the heart to ask her to go.

Left alone for a few minutes with her, I asked if she had ever sung on anything and she said no. She was extremely polite and courteous, and though she spoke in a low whisper that was barely audible, I was able to make out what she was saying. She politely asked me if she could satisfy me sexually. I politely refused.

She was dressed in rags. Her clothes were literally hanging off of her body. The crust around her ankles where the tops of her shoes would have been if she had been wearing any was solid black. I think she had one sock on and held on to what seemed to be her only possession, a blanket.

Her hooded sweatshirt might have been white or light grey when it was new and on a rack at a beautiful department store, but now it looked like someone tossed it on a barbeque grill. Z walked back in the door. I looked at him waiting for him to take her back outside, but instead he said, "Play her the track you just played me".

That girl, that sad, forlorn, beaten down girl, got up next to the microphone and sang one of the most beautiful and amazing songs I have ever heard. I played the synthesizer along with her and a guitar track I had already written was playing back, giving us a four bar melody at the slow tempo of a heartbeat to jam along to. She had an amazing and soulful voice, and she wrote the words as she sang them.

I was speechless.

Here was this woman who had been abused and raped her entire life, treated like an object for men to use so she could get crack to nullify the pain of her life, and she did this every day and every night for years and years and I cannot imagine what a lonely and miserable life that must be, I cannot imagine the pain she must have endured but I could not believe how absolutely beautiful her voice and words were.

After she finished the song and we did a second take without stopping, she pulled up her skirt and urinated in a red beer cup that was sitting near my sink. She placed the cup full of urine on top of my shelf above my keyboard and pulled a few garlands and plants out of her purse. She arranged them in a circle around the cup as if it were a Christmas decoration.

I went down the hall to a girl I know and bought her a pair of shoes.

CHAPTER FIFTY SEVEN

There are countless people down here who walk around not showering, not ever changing their clothes, not ever caring what they look like or how they smell, not caring if their underwear needs changing or if the bugs that crawl in their armpits and pubic hair could easily be taken care of with one dose of RID.

These are the real victims of Skid Row, the most vulnerable, most in need of help, and the most victimized by everyone. The thing about Skid Row is that they make almost no distinction between who really needs these services and who doesn't. Skid Row is meant to be a sort of halfway house for people who need to get their lives going again after being released from prison or jail or have been in a drug rehabilitation center.

It is NOT a place for people with permanent and incurable disabilities, though they live there in the thousands. Skid Row is NOT supposed to be populated with predators who know that this is where the weak and helpless are easy targets, though they come here to work without any opposition or fear. Skid Row is NOT supposed to be a pen in which big pharmaceutical companies are able to find human guinea pigs to test out their latest experimental drugs on.

Unfortunately, Skid Row is all of these things and more. I have been collecting stories and paperwork from people who have had very bad reactions to the drugs that they were given, and this practice of using society's most vulnerable members for research subjects is not only barbaric, but plain fucking evil. I've seen people I knew being rolled out of white vans after coming home from one of these experimental sessions, their eyes as big as saucers and some even still in hospital gowns. I'd have to walk them to their room or they would have fallen down in the middle of the street.

The women are able to get sanitary needs in many places, including the women's shelter, but too often I see them wiping the blood and excrement from between their legs and tossing it into the gutter only a few feet away from their tent. Some will try to keep it in a plastic bag and chastise those who don't, but the piles of fetid waste and stinking trash are never cleaned up by the homeless themselves even though they are only several feet away.

Instead, they will wait for the city to come by once every few weeks with bulldozers and hazmat suits, pack up as many of their things as they can carry, stuff their entire lives into shopping carts and wait on the next block while they disinfect the street. The entire tent city population for that block is uprooted and cramped on the next street, trying to keep whatever meager possessions they have from being stolen by everyone else as they sit on top of shopping carts filled to the brim with their lives and covered in blue plastic tarps while men scoop up their shit and rats explode out of the garbage piles in the streets and it never ends, it just gets moved from one part of town to another in an endless cycle of poverty, always with their mouths open, always with their hands stretched out for alms, and the men who grow the food and build the houses and create the jobs and own the factories look at the homeless and they see the same person every time, this homeless person, this person obviously back again looking for another handout, this person we gave, Didn't we give them a nice holiday something?

Only this isn't the same person, this person was still living in a house then, this is a brand new homeless person, one that the banks and the factories and the offices don't want any more and so that person falls down and down and down, always trying to catch a hand back up but fails and misses until they hit the bottom.

Some crash face first and some gently float down but when they arrive here they must wear the anonymous face of the homeless, the same face you see in every town in the United States, that same desperate look for help, that same cardboard sign on the freeway, that same last glimmer of hope that someone will give them steady work or a safe place to live or a clean change of clothes or protection from sexual assault or a bathroom that isn't filled with so much shit you must stand above it because sitting down is impossible or a good nights' sleep without bedbugs biting you or a friend to talk to or a cat or dog to keep and love forever..............

This is why I still live on Skid Row. I have never lived in a place where I've known every single person in my entire building. I have never felt so necessary and so appreciated for skills that I took for granted most of my life. I have never with such ease and speed been able to assist someone to the degree that their problem is solved and their smile is what I get in return (not counting the meals I get cooked for me on a daily basis, the knocks on my door with "YOU HUNGRY BABY? WE MAKIN SPAGHETTI COME EAT IF YOU WANT!") and meeting families on weekends eating slices of cake or pie every birthday and holiday, the hugs from old ladies who have no visitors, the love and support I get back from what I consider to be my family and my home are in abundance and even though the members slowly change over time, I get to know everyone as the new people eventually learn there's a white guy in the building and he will fix your computer or get you on the internet for free but you can kick him some herb once in a while and the gang bangers and Latino lovers and the old and infirm and mentally disabled and the terminally ill and the convicted felons all know they can knock on my door with a problem and I am good at solving problems and for this I am given a name.

BZB

That's my street name. The rappers that come into my recording studio would all be drinking and smoking while I was patching the effects boxes and setting compression levels, so they said I was 'The Busy Bee", so BZB I am, and hearing my beats from ghetto blasters every night as I walk down the street in Skid Row and get hellos and handshakes instead of spit and hate, people call my name and come running up with ideas and want to show me things and introduce me to people and record their songs with me and it's all wonderful. It really is.

But I can't stay here forever.

They need help.

It is impossible to try and remove the damage that living in one of these housing projects does to a person. They are so split sideways from the constant noise, the predatory dangers, the aggressive neighbors and late night partying and music that seems to randomly begin at 4:30 a.m., the noise, the NOISE, the fucking noise of helicopters going over and spotlights going past your window like it was a fucking concentration camp then as soon as it's quiet and you start to fall asleep that's when the bedbugs come and start to sting you bite you bedbugs don't mean you're a dirty person bedbugs mean you have warm blood and no matter what remedy you use or chemicals you spray one of your neighbors has them and they will be back soon enough you might get a week or three without incident but once they get a taste of you they will come back again and again and again and again keeping you from sleeping and making sure you stay an alarmed and stressed person.

To combat bedbugs I tried everything, even weirdo contraptions on Youtube. Nothing worked. I finally gave up and built a hammock inside of my apartment. It keeps the bedbugs off but now my back hurts from sleeping like a giant scrotum. I Installed it badly, seven feet in the air like an idiot (Hooks in proper studs, but I forgot a hammock doesn't pull down, it pulls IN) and sent me sprawling to the floor where a five inch nail went through my arm and another grazed my skull.

I mean that's pretty much a standard day in Skid Row. Someone's always coming out of jail with some teeth missing, or beating on their wife or girlfriend in the hallway, being followed by police or having the health department show up with a complaint. It's non stop, but it's no place to raise children, and it's no place for adults who are in rehabilitation.

Drugs of every kind are right outside of my front door, and often people knock and hand me a package just for the fuck of it. I've been clean eight years this November so I've been putting the baggies away and I have a nice little stash if anyone wants it.

CHAPTER FIFTY EIGHT

The next day I overslept and got to the spot at 5th and Broadway about 6:15 a.m.. No one was around. No one. I walked the block and turned on 6th street to see every single person I knew lined up against the wall with handcuffs on. I keep walking like I was on my way to work and I can tell by the way the police cars were lined up they just arrived five minutes earlier.

I saw junkies poke their heads out here and there, spot me and IMMEDIATELY start towards me. I panicked and started to run because the police were going to see all of those addicts starting to follow me and I had two packs, the ONLY two packs, and they were not going to give up on me easily. We got about a block away and I sold a few guys a few balloons to get rid of the crowd but others were in hot pursuit.

I looked over to the other side of the street and saw the pack man in a garage waving me towards him. He had escaped. So had I.

Eleven dealers were arrested in all, pretty much shutting down the heroin trade for the day, except they didn't get me and they didn't get the pack man. I sent a scout to look for customers and slowly brought them a few blocks away one at a time from the main strip.

I gave everyone my phone number and told them to meet me at a bus stop a few blocks away, no strangers, do not run up to me holding cash out or I will cut you off. Walk slow and be patient. One customer after the other, slowly and carefully, I collected more and more cash.

By the time the day was over, I had given over seventy five daily users my number.

I sold about twenty two hundred dollars worth of dope that day and made six hundred dollars for myself.

I was about to level up.

All of the customers were mine.

End of part one.

The rear cover of this book shows the burn marks on a wall on the corner of 5th and Gladys where a woman had been murdered by being rolled up in her tent and set on fire.

Photo taken by the author.